MY PLEDGE!

The Power of Prayer

MY PLEDGE!

The Power of Prayer

*Be Victorious in Every situation
Inspirational Poems, Testimonies*

Fyne C. Ogonor

© 2020 by Fyne C. Ogonor
Fyneauthor@gmail.com
www.FyneOgonor.com
Published by:
Ronval International, LLC
Atlanta, Georgia, USA
Info@ronvalinternational.com
www.ronvalinternational.com

Formerly published as "My Pledge! What's Yours?"
Copyright 2018 by Fyne C. Ogonor

All rights reserved solely by the author. The author guarantees all contents are original and do not infringe upon the legal rights of any other person or work. No part of this book may be reproduced in any form without the permission of the author.

Unless otherwise indicated, Scripture quotations taken from the New King James Version (NKJV). Copyright © 1982 by Thomas Nelson, Inc. Used by permission. All rights reserved.

ISBN Softcover: 978-1-951460-11-2
ISBN E Book: 978-1-951460-12-9
Library of Congress Control Number: 2018909373

Published and Printed in the U.S.A.

Dedication

I dedicate this book, *My Pledge!*, first, to my late parents, Elder Judah U. Kakoro and Mrs. Fester Judah, for the light they put in my hands to illuminate my path. Also, I dedicate this book to my five wonderful and amazing children, Valerie, Ronald, Bryan, Jessica, and Stephanie. Your cheering and support inspire me to do more. Thank you. I pray my heavenly Father keeps on showering you with His love, favor, and blessings in Jesus' name. May our God protect and guide you always. May He bless your endeavors, prosper you in health, wealth and long life. And let our Lord endow you with His uncommon wisdom in Jesus name. Amen. I love you all with all my heart. Most importantly, thank you for your friendship.

Inaddition, I want to dedicate this book to all the children I have been privileged to serve over the years. They have touched my life in a special way to become a better person. Learning and growing with them has broadened my knowledge and wisdom in my perceptions about matters of life. As you scatter in this world, may you be like the seeds planted by the riverbank, blossom, be fruitful, and become a force to be reckoned with in your environment. Also, I thank all the saints of God that have been praying for me, my family and my ministry.

Finally, in all my accomplishments, I give to God the Almighty, all the glory, honor, and adoration, through my Savior, Jesus Christ. Amen.

Acknowledgments

First, I thank the Almighty God for making this book project possible. May His name alone be praised. Also, I want to thank Elder, Dr. Tom Carter and his wife for their love and encouragement. I especially thank Elder Carter for his honest critique of this script, being an author himself.

Furthermore, I thank my daughter, Valerie Ogonor, for typesetting and proofreading of some of the scripts. Particularly, Val, I very much appreciate your tireless efforts on guiding me on technology matters. In addition, I want to express my gratitude to my son Bryan Ogonor and my husband, Vincent Ogonor, for helping me type some of the scripts.

I also thank Pastor Fredrick A. Russell for taking the time, despite his busy schedule, to review my script. May God continue to bless your ministry. In Jesus' name. Amen.

Finally, I want to thank Deborah Perdue of Illumination Graphics, who did such a great job on the interior design. And for all relatives, friends, and others that had anything to do with this book, directly or indirectly, from first draft to the final script, I say thank you. May God bless every one of you in Jesus' name. Amen.

TABLE OF CONTENTS

FOREWORD BY DR. G. TOM CARTER x
Minister and Attorney

PROLOGUE
The Message 1
A life without a purpose is not worth living

CHAPTER ONE
An Invitation to a pledge of service 5

CHAPTER TWO
A Child Asks, Who Can Change My Tomorrow Today? . 11
A child's learning experience starts from the home

CHAPTER THREE
My Foundation 15
"Train up a child in the way he should go,…"

CHAPTER FOUR
Balancing between two cultures 29
To be different is uniqueness

CHAPTER FIVE 33
A Time to be born, and a time to die
Glorify God in every situation

CHAPTER SIX
The Unforgettable Lesson 39
Child-Parent Spiritual Connection {CPSC}

CHAPTER SEVEN
The Belief Principle 45
Your Beliefs, not your circumstances, determine your peace and happiness
Testimony One: When your heart is bitter 46
Testimony Two: The essence of memory 52
Testimony Three: The turning point 56
Testimony Four: A mother's prayer 61

CHAPTER EIGHT
Putting Belief To Work! 65
Belief is a choice

CHAPTER NINE
The Power of Prayer 69
Prayer is a response to God's call

CHAPTER TEN
Testimony Five —Intercessory prayer in action 73
Don't pray just for yourselves, pray for one another

CHAPTER ELEVEN
Testimony Six — The Devil's Midnight Visit 85
"No weapon fashioned against you shall prosper."

CHAPTER TWELVE
Testimony Seven —The Graduation Ceremony. 91
Light up your candles today so your tomorrow will be illuminated

CHAPTER THIRTEEN
Reaching outside the box 99
All children belong to God

CHAPTER FOURTEEN
Dare to Believe, My God is Real! 111
"If God is for us, who can be against us?"

CHAPTER FIFTEEN 119
EPILOGUE
Standing on God's Promises

REFERENCES. 124

AUTHOR'S PROFILE. 125

STORIES IN PICTURES
The Graduation Ceremony 126
Growing up and COHISA Days 128
Bye Bye Africa. 130
Hello America! 131
1st COHISA Worldwide Convention 134

Foreword

Fyne Ogonor has allowed us to see a unique insight into what life is all about. Being deeply immersed in both the cultures of Nigeria and the United States of America, she shows how hard work, wise planning, providential circumstances and most of all her personal relationship with God have enabled her to achieve her vision.

The book is sprinkled with real-life experiences that richly illustrate the values she seeks to portray. Her experiences include being delivered miraculously from death at a point of a gun to amazing scholastic achievements in both the United States and Nigeria.

Fyne Ogonor is both a business entrepreneur and philanthropist. She has started businesses in both Nigeria and the United States.

Especially noteworthy is her work in the education of children, giving them a new lease on life. I have had the privilege of knowing Fyne Ogonor and her husband, Vincent Ogonor, for some seventeen years. We need this book to see the Divine purpose of our lives, and to commit ourselves to reaching higher.

G. Tom Carter Minister and Attorney

Prologue

THE MESSAGE

A life without a purpose is not worth living

The question is, how does your unspoken message impact the environment where you exist and the people in it?

Wherever you find yourself to serve, whether in working for a paycheck as a means of making a living, or an assignment in the house of God, it's a privilege. Therefore, give it nothing but your best. Don't look behind you to see who is watching; because the one who packaged you and dropped you there is looking down to see if you are serving the purpose in which you're sent there for or not. Be not alarmed to dis-cover that sometimes some people would reject the message and fight against your existence. When this happens, call on your maker and say, help me Lord!

In difficult situations, without God's strength and His calm whisper to the heart, it would be impossible to stand up to the enemies who want to destroy the message. The enemy can cause a dislike and/or a misunderstanding of what the message stands for, especially if you are in a leading position. If you are a leader, you are the servant to the people; be a servant leader. Know that God is watching you, and do right by Him.

For His grace brings obedience to the heart to remain and serve in a hostile environment until the package is opened and message read by all concerned.

Persistence is important even when the message is not embraced, the memory of the unspoken message to the witnesses becomes a legacy that will live-on in that environment, and in their hearts, whether they accept you and the message or not.

In a nutshell, it's beneficial to always look up to Jesus as our boss, because in the end, the only evaluation that matters, is that of our Lord's.

Moreover, in order to succeed in showcasing the growth of the great seed inside of you to blossom, you need an unquestionable golden passion, coated with ability, and embellished with confidence. These are the ultimate natural invisible credentials that will discover your voice, and give you the boldness and permission to sing your song for the world to hear; and witness your trail of legacy.

Your voice has no duplicate, express it as loud as you can with great passion. The world yearns to hear you sing. What are you waiting for? Put on your robe of confidence, hop on the stage of life, and illuminate your environment with your light. The world is watching you. More importantly, your creator is watching what you'd do with your destiny. Remember, you are a representative of the Creator-God, on planet Earth. Don't disappoint the world; don't disappoint God; and, don't disappoint yourself. Be the best you, you can be.

In order to succeed in showcasing the growth of the great seed inside of you to blossom, you need an unquestionable golden passion, coated with ability, and embellished with confidence.

Chapter One

AN INVITATION TO A PLEDGE OF SERVICE

This book, *My Pledge!* was motivated from my real-life experiences and observations. First, I want my readers to know how thankful I am for God guiding my thoughts, plans, and actions. Secondly, I want to convey to every parent, teacher and guardian how important it is to cooperate with God in giving every child the opportunity to have and fulfill their dreams. Thirdly, I want to challenge everyone of you to do your part in helping not only your immediate family but also the desperately needy children of the world. These too are God's children and thus our children.

Also, discover the secret to living a blissful life on a lighted path conquering the invading darkness of this world.

THE PLEDGE!
An invitation to a pledge of service

Chapter One

THE EDUCATOR

All Shepherds

Almighty God, I thank You for Your grace and blessings.
For the bundle of talents, you've bestowed in me,
I pledge to use all within my capacity,
to impart knowledge to the growing children;
To make a difference in humanity,
Reflecting Your light in the World.
Therefore Father, grant me the wisdom
to implement and share the gifts according to Your will.
Amen.

THE PARENT

All Caregivers/Guardians

For the love of God,
I promise to care, love, and protect my child
with all my heart and soul.
I will do the best I can within my ability to provide
for his academic needs.
I will cherish his teachers and his school,
Working in unity to make a difference in a life that will
influence tomorrow.
Lord, grant me the courage, patience, and endurance to do
all I can in your name.
Amen.

Chapter One

THE STUDENT

All Youth Scholars

With the love of God,
I promise to do my best to honor my parents, teachers,
and my God.
As a student, I will work hard to earn my grades.
As a future leader, I will aspire to live an exemplary life.
I will obey my seniors, love and protect my juniors,
and remain friendly to my peers.
Help me Lord to walk according to Your footsteps.
Amen.

My Pledge!

Children, light up your candles today so your tomorrow will be illuminated . . . You cannot achieve without knowing how to learn, and you cannot lead if you cannot learn. Learning produces good leadership. Remember this: a life without a purpose is not worth living.

Chapter Two

A CHILD ASKS: WHO CAN CHANGE MY TOMORROW TODAY?

A child's learning experience starts from the home

I believe that every human being on Earth has a purpose, a God-given purpose to deliver and accomplish on Earth.

God has given each individual a specific assignment, and has created us in a special way. In order to achieve God's purpose for our lives, we must learn, grow, and mature physically, mentally, and spiritually.

A child's behavior can be influenced positively or negatively by several factors within his environment, such as family, friends, teachers, church, the community, school, social class, and the world in general. However, children are most influenced by the people whom they see, hear, and listen to. These people are parents, siblings, teachers, and their peers. It is very vital to impart positive thinking and good behavior in a child at an early stage and to influence him positively in every aspect of life through adulthood.

Hence, parents should be the first set of people to encourage their children to dream. A dream is a goal that gives direction, organization, and purpose. I believe God has created every human being with a seed of greatness. You can water it to blossom, or you can wither it down. Children's aspirations and desires must be encouraged by people who are influential in their life.

A child's learning experience starts from the home. Parents should create an environment that makes a child feel secured, safe, and loved. It will help to build their confidence and self-esteem. For many years, research has proven over and over that children who grow up with love and kindness, will reflect such to others and become happy people.

Teachers are the second group of people that should influence a child positively, because most children look up to their teachers as role models. One of the obligations of teachers in a child's life is to nurture the child's dream, and to never dismiss or discourage his/her desires and aspirations.

Furthermore, the biggest assets for every growing child should be determination and resilience. Hence, the recipe for a child's achievement in life is: Parental encouragement to dream dreams, teachers nurturing the talents to bring the dream alive, and a child's determination and resilience to succeed. All these put together will produce a human being that

CHAPTER TWO

is ready to serve his/her God-given purpose on Earth; *and certainly, success will follow.* The word of God confirms this in **Proverbs 22:6**— *"Train up a child in the way he should go, and when he is old he will not depart from it."*

Children, light up your candles today so your tomorrow will be illuminated. Cherish what your parents and your teachers can give you. You cannot achieve without knowing how to learn, and you cannot lead if you cannot learn. Learning produces good leadership. Remember this, **a life without a purpose is not worth living.**

Chapter Three

MY FOUNDATION

Who is this Woman?

Some of you may be asking, who is this woman? Is she qualify to tell me about God? By the world's standard, probably not. However, my heavenly Father, through the grace of our Lord Jesus, has given me the privilege of telling the world the story of love and hope. The story that reveals God's promises and faithfulness; reminding every child of God— every human created by God, of His goodness. I can assure you by my personal experience that "our God is real".

GROWING UP

*"Train up a child in the way he should go,
And when he is old he will not depart from it."*

This book is not my autobiography nor is it about my ministry. However, I want to share with you a little bit about my foundation.

I was born of two wonderful parents—Elder Judah U. Kakoro and Mrs. Fester Judah. Both from Odiokwu village in Ahoada West Local Government Area, Rivers State, Nigeria. They were avid farmers, as farming is the way of life in the village.

Professionally, my father was a renowned tailor in the Ekpeye Kingdom. He designed and made clothing for men, women, old and young. He trained several professional Fashion Designers/Tailors in the area. In addition to tailoring, he worked in the Lord's vineyard. His evangelical ministry availed him the opportunity to travel to other places to spread the word of God.

Also, my father, with the help of my mother, established other businesses such as a retail store, a poultry and goat farm at home. In addition, after he settled at home, a palm produce

Chapter Three

production which is a small-scale industry, was added to his business enterprises. Although, my parents were blessed with seven children, I was closest with three brothers—two older and one younger. My two older sisters had left home, one before I was born and the other when I was very little; my parents lost one child.

Growing up, there was no time our household did not shelter and feed fifteen or more people at a time—including apprentices and relatives. And my parents never played favorites in dealing with us. In my family, hard work was the unspoken way of life.

My parents were not financially rich, but they had spiritual wealth. Our home was filled with joy and laughter. A lot of the lessons I learned from my parents as a child, have helped me with my belief system—what life is all about. I have summarized the many lessons they taught me, directly or indirectly which has influenced the way I live, as the stories and testimonies in this book will unfold, into 20 life principle nuggets, plus one.

1. Kindness is loving and caring.
2. There is no impossibility in life; the only limitation is the one you set for yourself.
3. Not everyone will love you, just keep loving anyway.
4. For all phases of life, be in agreement with God before you proceed.
5. Never forget where you started; but don't be stagnant, broaden your horizon.
6. The appearance of the clouds—life challenges, should never stop you from moving forward.

7. Put on the shield of God always before any journey; the spiritual wars are never announced: Satan is always ready to attack.

8. Open no doors for fear, doubt, and anxiety; rely on the undefeated general, our Lord Jesus Christ, who is always ahead of you.

9. Just because you're doing everything right does not mean the whole crowd will hail you. There are always people who will view you as an enemy no matter what you do. Don't be discouraged by criticisms; be right with God and do your best.

10. Life comes with the good, the bad and the ugly, but your choices determine your destination.

11. Never fuel your mind with inferiority; you're as good and qualified as anybody to handle the responsibility God gives you.

12. Humility opens an invitation door to dine with the King at the dinner table. But boldness inserts the confidence that permits you to join in the dinner discussion.

13. When you eat, remember there are others somewhere wishing for a little portion of that food to survive. Pray, that they receive meals too.

14. Tripping and falling does not mean your legs are weak; refusing to get up makes you a cripple.

15. Embrace Gratitude. Cheerfully say thank you; compliment with lavishing praises without exaggeration.

16. It's okay if you don't succeed when you try; but refusing to try again is a failure.

17. All things are possible in life, only when you put your faith in God.

18. When you soak yourself in the presence of God, "no weapon fashioned against you shall prosper."

19. In every crises, there's a lesson to be learned; as there is light at the end of a tunnel.

20. For every good deed, direct the glory to God, for the praises of men cannot take you to heaven.

While my dad was evangelizing in public, my mother was evangelizing at home. Every location and situation was a den or haven for mother's heavenly stories. Today, I am very appreciative of my parents—for the composition of who they were. The way I was brought up, especially the light they carried that illuminated my path, to guide me through the journey of life.

When I was in elementary school, I thought my dad was always reading the bible due to lack of other books to read. I never really looked at it as the book of life or as our life's instructional manual. In my early years, I thought the bible was for church only and family devotion—that's it.

The word of God is our key and power. No matter how bad you think a situation is, don't panic, hold on to the word of God. Keep your eyes on the Lord even when you cannot reach His hand, grab His garment and the power from Him will bless you with a miracle. What does this mean, you ask? This means you have a direct line of communication with God in the name of our Savior Jesus Christ. It doesn't matter where you've been; when you call, He will hear you; and meet you at the point of your needs.

CAREER ADVANTAGE

Pursuing a dream requires more than credential qualifications.

*I*n the first place, I pledge my allegiance to the Almighty God for life, His grace and favors.

In a special way, I extend my gratitude to the United States of America for the opportunity afforded me to achieve an all-round education with practical experiences in matters of survival skills. It is a fact that discrimination exists anywhere human beings are found. The U.S.A. is not an exception. However, professionally, my experience in the United States of America is very positive. What I know of the American culture, if you can deliver, you got it— no matter your color or gender. This is to say that generally, if you have the qualifications and experiences required of a job, you'll be hired without discrimination. On this note, I want to use this opportunity to acknowledge some people who opened the door and dropped the ladder of career success for me.

Chapter Three

First, I want to express my gratitude to Mr. Larry Elliot who opened the door of the Hyatt Regency for me to work in my field of study while I was still in college for my Bachelor's degree program. Working as an office attendant afforded me the exposure of knowing a little bit of every department within the organization. Especially, the exposure of learning about customer service.

My course mates and some of my schoolmates and friends used to envy me each time I'd leave school for work—particularly the African students like me. They called me the lucky one. They call it luck, but I call it God's favor, considering the fact that I was given a special schedule to accommodate my classes. When I went for the second interview and I told Gerald, my immediate supervisor, and the department manager, about my classes, he took me to the General Manager, Mr. Elliot. "Can you work 4 PM to 12 Mid Night and still be able to attend your 8:00 AM class?" he asked. "Yes Sir!" I responded.

Once I started working there, the company paid part of my school fees; part of my semester credit hours tuition yearly—as included in my benefit package. Gerald, wherever you are, thank you.

The opportunity they extended to me was also a blessing to the organization—God's grace upon my life allowed my light to shine in that environment. For example, in less than ten months of my working there, I became an employee of the month among hundreds of employees.

After acquiring my Bachelor's degree, coming out into the world, my Superstar status from Hyatt Regency gave me invaluable access to job opportunities, including the starting of my own businesses.

Why am I telling this story? It is a story of encouragement. It takes boldness and confidence to go for what some people disqualify themselves for, because of status quo. I had four things that could have worked against me if I decided to limit myself. 1) I am a woman 2) a black person 3) a foreigner and 4) a student.

I excelled from lower to middle management in corporate America; and later a president and CEO of my own company—until the call. America for sure, is a land of opportunity; for those with big dreams, anything is possible.

Chapter Three

MY FOUNDATION

As I excelled in the leadership ladder, I involuntarily acquired some nicknames as in the way others around me perceive me. Names such as:

- The Velvet Hammer,
- Seasoned Administrator,
- Margaret Thatcher,
- The American Woman,
- The Iron Lady, and
- The Prayer woman, who knows what else I'm not aware of yet.

The Velvet Hammer: by some of my employees in one of my early management jobs after my Bachelor's degree. A Hispanic lady one day asked me, "Ms. Fyne, why are they calling you Velvet Hammer? Who calls me Velvet Hammer?" I asked. She laughed. Then I asked her, "what is velvet hammer?" "I don't know," she responded. For not knowing what it meant, I was a little troubled. I entered an analytical segment of myself;

an analysis of others' perception of me. I started with my superiors, all I kept hearing were their compliments of a good job, excellent job, etc. Then I came to my colleagues, and I realized I had a great rapport with everyone. However, a bell kept ringing in my head of a particular scene; I just came in for work one morning, as I entered the lobby I looked on my right, I saw two front desk clerks at the reception, I greeted them with a wave. Momentarily, I heard "hey Ms. Fyne." I looked on my left, coming from one of the banquet halls was one of the Supervisors. I responded to his greetings; out of the blue he said, "you're exhilarated, you really like this job, don't you?" I smiled and responded, "yea" with a head nod.

The next day, we both met again in the accounting office. I don't know if it was a coincidence or if he came there because he saw me. What's your secret?" He then looked at the front desk manager and said, with his finger pointing at me, "how does she do it? Do what" I asked; "how do you keep on smiling, even when everybody else is stressed out, you keep on smiling. What's your secret?" I did not know how to respond nor what to say. This was one of the few times in my life that words refused to flow out of my mouth on the stage of communication. I shrugged my shoulders and left the scene. If it were now, I would have understood where he was coming from; and give him some words of hope. Obviously, even though we were both working for the same organization, we were not at the same level of passion.

In other words, a passion for a job determines your level of stress; you can be busy with little or no stress.

Finally, on the Velvet hammer, I analyzed down to the employees under me. As a human being, I was very much

Chapter Three

aware I wasn't perfect; but I could not visibly see any negative situation that reflected or even implied unhappiness in my department; because my exhilarating mode was contagious— we had a lot of laughter, and team spirit. At the end, I decided I'd not spend one more moment thinking about it.

In about a week later, a letter from the general manager, Mike Reads:

Dear Fyne Ogonor,

"I am writing to let you know that your Pickett pride is showing. And you are therefore invited to a banquette in your honor as one of the winners of the PHCER award— the award of excellence for this year." The selection process for this award:

1) By my Superiors

2) By my peers— my fellow management colleagues

3) By my employees.

I was really humbled by it, and suddenly, searching for the meaning of that nickname didn't matter anymore; it couldn't be that bad after all, I concluded.

Seasoned Administrator: By two of my former principals I employed at different times. One of them was an expatriate.

They're both older than myself, more experienced and both professional Educators. Yet, they welcomed some fresh and new ideas I brought to the table, which they considered useful and very helpful in their day to day decision making. I was truly humbled by it, because they said it to me, and both qualified their statements with different meanings. The credible compliments, from such distinguished caliber of people, gave me a reassurance of my services to humanity.

Margret Thatcher: As a young girl, I heard about Mrs. Margaret Thatcher of United Kingdom, a Prime Minister, a woman I highly respect; powerful British woman with high integrity. Someone I would have loved to know personally.

A group of Educators, private school owners, whom I served as their Chair Person for five years, honorably gave me that nickname without my knowledge. As I later found out this name was given to me right from my first tenure; but it never got to my ears until my fourth year of serving them.

After a summer holiday, I convened a meeting of my executives in my office and I asked about a report —an appointed committee ought to have given to them while I was overseas, United States of America. One of the Executive members said, "Ma there's no report." "Why?" "They said they will not give any report until Margaret Thatcher comes back." "Who is Margaret Thatcher?" They all looked at each other and laughed. "Oh, I see! So, I'm the Margaret Thatcher?" Then I turned to my Secretary and I said, "call the Chairman of that committee and tell him that Margaret Thatcher is back, and they should schedule to give their report."

Whether I earned these names people call me or not, I cannot say; however, I receive them as others' evaluation of me. At the end, I am who I am. And I sincerely hope that I am living to be the person God has created me to be, and serving the purpose which He sent me to planet earth.

Chapter Three

Wherever I find myself, I try to leave a positive mark; something that will make people say, when she was with us, or during her time this or that would have been handled this way….

In summary, utilize every opportunity to create a new path and leave a trail, others can follow.

Chapter Four

BALANCING BETWEEN TWO CULTURES

To be different is uniqueness

As I stated earlier, I am a daughter of a Bible teacher, Preacher, and an entrepreneur, who has the privilege of living in two different cultures. Balancing the two cultures sometimes is challenging.

Leaving West Africa for the U.S.A., I experienced a culture shock. That was normal; besides, I had just moved on from the classic teenage stage to early adulthood. Leaving behind the stable nest of my parents' home for adventuring to a world unknown as my own life manager was difficult enough. But adding the change in the weather, food, language and the total difference in culture was like diving from a very high mountain to a valley without any slope. I included language because, even though I studied English in Africa, the different accent made it seem like a language I was not familiar with. But my young age helped me to adjust within a short time.

However, what doesn't make much sense to me is returning to Africa after being away for about twenty-five years, and experiencing a culture shock. This time, it was worse than my American Culture shock. Unexpected? Yes. Ridiculous?

Not really.

I went back to Africa with the teenage mentality—assuming the world was stagnant. Living there as an adult, I experienced a clash of cultures—the one I grew up as a child to teenager, and the one I grew up as teenage/young adult to adulthood.

Despite the differences, the advantages outweighed the disadvantages; because I had the choice to choose the better of both cultures to apply to my everyday living.

For instance, I stated earlier about the nicknames my associates, employees, and students called me. Every name as mentioned in the previous chapter signify strength in leadership, a learned trait I acquired from my American culture; attention to details, ability to listen and making decisions without wavering.

On the other hand, I inherited natural leadership ability from my father. This comes from boldness, a positive self-esteem and assertiveness! I call it inherited because it was normal for me. My father was my role model as he absorbed us into his businesses, and his ministry.

Beyond this, the reflection of confidence that others see, comes from my relationship with God—putting Him in

Chapter Four

charge in all that I do, and trusting Him. Again, this is one of the lessons I learned from my parents.

Now, let me give you two examples of how I choose the best of the two cultures. In America, title is not a big deal. It's okay for a young person to call an adult by his/her first name. Whereas, in my African culture, you would not dare call your senior by his/her first name. You must address them by sir/madam, uncle/auntie, daddy/mommy, even when they are not related to you. Most people have titles such as Chief, Engineer, Doctor, Barrister, etc. Africans value titles. I do not feel right with the American way; so, no matter where I find myself, I never address or call those old enough to be my parents, by their first names. Also, I made sure my children follow the African culture on this.

Another conflict was whether to look directly into a person's face. My African culture demands when a senior is talking to a junior, the younger person—the junior looks down as a sign of respect.

Personally, I have problem with that, looking down seems more like a disrespect to me. I go with my American culture on this. If I'm talking to a child, I want him/her to look straight in my eyes— when he lies, I'd know. But looking down? No, it doesn't work.

I hope the little I have talked about my foundation has helped my readers who don't know me to know a little about me. And for those around me who should know me but really don't. I hope this will help you understand where I'm coming from.

In Africa, very often I'd hear, "that is not for this culture, it will only apply or work in the western world". Directly or indirectly they see me as a foreigner. But in other instances, some individuals would expect me to behave and appear exactly like them. It cannot be. I am an individual; I cannot be like anybody else but myself. Furthermore, my lifestyle is influenced by two cultures and I thank God for that. Although I love my two cultures, I pray that Jesus remains my standard and not any tradition or culture. The bottom line is that I must be the best 'me' I can be—looking up to Jesus as I prepare for my eternal home.

In fact, we are all made to be unique in some way. I love forging a non-existing path, forming a trail, others can use; living a legacy.

Chapter Five

A TIME TO BE BORN, AND A TIME TO DIE...

Glorify God in every situation

It was the year 1998 when the familiar pain of losing a family member re-emerged. The pain of losing a parent was no stranger to me; only this time I was no longer a teenager. No matter the age, it's a feeling that leaves a big hole in one's heart; a hole that, through time can heal, but never can it be sealed.

At 11:49 PM September 14, 1998, a childhood lesson was retrieved from my memory—gratitude to God in all things and for all things. No matter the situation, we must always give praises to God for His goodness. When we showcase an attitude of a grateful heart, not only will it ease our pains, it will be planted in the hearts of our children. Children embrace the modeled behavior of their parents. On this note I wrote:

I am starting a gratitude journal today because I have realized that I do not thank my God enough nor praise Him as often as I ought to. He has blessed me abundantly more than I can enumerate, nor deserve. As from this moment, I'm going to start counting my blessings from God. This is a way to remind me how blessed I really am, no matter what the enemy says or does, I know my heavenly Father loves me very much.

Earlier this evening, while at work, I called my friend Ayo. She asked about my going home with the kids for my father's burial. I responded, "I still plan to go with them, but at this moment, I do not know how possible, financially speaking. However, I believe and have faith that God will provide." Then Ayo made an interesting statement that whatever I plan to do, that I always succeed.

Driving home from work, Ayo's statement occupied my thoughts so much that I stopped by a Walmart department store to pick up a journal. "What does her statement mean?" I thought. It means that God is always there to see me through my thoughts, plans, and actions.

Is God's favorable response to my needs, because of my faith in Him? Yes, to an extent, but it's more of His grace and favor upon my life. He showers His undeserving grace on me, and I receive it. Thank you, Lord Jesus. Thank you, God. Finally, I pledged to write five things or more that I thank God for, each day.

My gratitude inspiration Led to the birth of this poem:

Chapter Five

My Plea!

Give me the strength O Lord!

To do the things I have to do.

Give me the Courage to run

The extra mile to get to my destination.

Give me an open mind;

To see and tackle things objectively.

Give me a level eye,

Knowledge to understand,

And wisdom to act and react wisely.

Thank You Lord, for Thy blessings. Amen.

I concluded my journaling for that night with these gratitude points:

1) Thank you God for watching over me and my family.
2) Thank You for making me realize how blessed I am through my friend Ayo.
3) Thank You for giving me the strength to complete my two jobs today.
4) Thank You Lord for providing us with this home; our own house.
5) I Thank God for my husband and my children...Thank You Jesus.

And each night my daily activities ended by writing five gratitude points in my gratitude journal.

The question remains, was my friend accurate in her perception of me? "That whatever I plan to do, I always succeed?" Logically and ideally yes, her perception was correct.

Practically, it is very far from the truth. I do not succeed or achieve in whatever I touch or want. But I strongly cling unto God to lead my way. So even when things don't work out, I strongly believe that it wasn't the will of God anyway. And that He has something better for me. I don't say it to put on a show; rather, I say it because I believe it. This belief in my inner self, sends out a positive message of confidence in God, and this is what my friend perceived, and her interpretation was success.

Despite my solid faith in God, this is how I saw myself before Ayo's statement: A struggling career woman who works 24/6 to make ends meet. And a devoted mother and wife who takes care of everybody but has no time for herself.

Even people who have faith in God, occasionally experience spiritual let down. And for me this is one of those times. I had invested every dime I had in this universe in the process of acquiring a house, where my children could call home. Shortly after that, I had the news of my father being asleep in the Lord. My hope was paralyzed momentarily; because I had no money to go home nor for the funeral expenses, not to mention going with some of my children, especially the last three that didn't really have the opportunity to meet one of the most important persons in their existence, whom I have told them some wonderful stories about. I felt the need of the

Chapter Five

kids being part of the ceremony to have closure. Even though they did not have the opportunity to spend time with him while alive, but at least they can witness his farewell on his exit from this Earth.

I calculated my monthly income from both my management job and my second job, yet going home with my kids was not a viable option. Still, I refused to give up on the idea. My faith activated hope that produced spiritual energy within me, to persistently petition to God. And at the end of each prayer I would thank Him for the miracle I was expecting from Him, granting of my request.

While at work, I was too busy to worry about my personal problems. I was either training people on how to do their jobs right, and advising customers or helping them on image enhancement. At the same time, I was actively involved in my five children's school and church activities. All of them were in primary, middle, and high school age. They were all very active in deferent activities. And I'm the type that didn't want to miss anything unless it's unavoidable. I feel kid's activities is a process of creating memories for them, and our quality time together.

At home, I was a housewife and my motherly chores continued. Both my jobs and my home duties compelled me to talk and take care of everyone cheerfully despite my emotional state of mind. In the whole process, there was one person I did not have much time for, myself. Sometimes we get so involved in the drama of this universe that we lose touch with ourselves. And sometimes we disconnect our antenna from God, which affects our communication channel to Him.

Stop for a moment; ask yourself what really matters in your life? Look inside the universe, where is your location? And what is your purpose on Earth? Are you paying attention to God's instructions? Or are you still waiting for the instructional manual for your divine purpose? Be still, and listen. God is speaking today, as He did yesterday, and He will tomorrow. Make time for yourself, and especially make time for God. A quiet time with God will help you find yourself in the universe, and discover or rediscover the goodness of our Lord.

Faith is not enough when there is no constant spiritual nourishment with the word of God to prevent spiritual let down. But faith that is fortified by the holy word of God produces immunity that can repel fear, anxiety and doubt.

Chapter Six

THE UNFORGETTABLE LESSON

Child-Parent Spiritual Connection (CPSC)

One Faithful-afternoon, I was in a seminar class on my marketing job; a class of almost one hundred employees, each with a computer terminal. We all had a training manual that we used to input information into the computer system. The instructor would instruct how to input page after page of data.

I remember vividly, after a specific exercise, there was a question from the audience, so after explaining, she said "now flip to page . . . , and on your keyboard, key in…," instead of seeing the result she told us we would see, I saw my father lying like a dead body on a bed that looked like a hospital bed. I froze. I could still hear everything the instructor was saying. As I stared at my monitor screen tears started gushing from my eyes. I sat on the first lane on the left, facing the instructor, and on the second row from the front. I looked on the two terminals in front of me; they had same information as we were told. The young man next to me asked, "are you alright?" As I said yes; I looked on his monitor, it had the same thing others had. Then he looked at my monitor, my monitor was blank. The picture disappeared. "What happened to your system?"

"I don't know," I responded. I excused myself and went out. I could not continue with the training, so I left for home.

As I got home, I called my husband at work and told him what I saw. He was pretty shaken by it saying "that's not good. We can't handle that now." Financially, we were not in a good place. I tried calling my home country repeatedly but all to no avail. I called a family friend of ours in another state in the U. S., and I told him my experience. He was dumbfounded by the unusual situation. He advised that I should keep on calling until I got through.

Finally, I got through to my godmother, and she assured me nothing was wrong, because she and my godfather, her husband, visited my dad like two days ago she said. They went for a church meeting and they stopped by the house that evening. "Papa entertained us very well and he was very healthy and happy." She reported. I really wanted to accept that and let go, but in my spirit, I felt the contrary. Therefore, I requested that she send for my younger brother and inquire if all was well.

Moments later, my children came back from school and I gathered them and said, we need to pray for grandpa; we held hands in a circle and prayed. I kept on trying till it was

Chapter Six

too late over there. About our 2 AM, I started again till 6 AM our time. Still the circuit was busy. I took a break to get the kids ready for school. One of my girls asked, "Mom, have you heard anything yet?" "Not yet." I responded. "Mom, why don't we pray again? Should I call everybody so we can pray?" "That's okay, sweetheart, I don't want you kids to be late for school." I finished styling her hair as others left, she turned back and said, "Hold my hands, let's pray, I'll pray." So, her prayer went like this: "Father God, please console my mom. Also, open the phone line so she can find out about my grandpapa, In Jesus' Name. Amen."

As soon as I kissed her goodbye, I closed the door and went straight to the phone, one dial, the phone went through. My godmother was as if she was sitting by the phone. As she answered, she exclaimed "oh Fyne!" I knew something was wrong. Then she said, "your younger brother just walked in." I found out from him, my father was in a coma. The medicine that doctor prescribed was not available in any pharmacy store within the town and even in the state capital city. Up to that moment—second day afternoon, nothing was given to my father as treatment. He fell and hit his head, and nothing was done for two days, no medication in the hospital. With the help of my godparents, they had sent someone to the commercial city outside our state. Then sad news: By the time the medicine to be used in the I.V. arrived, it was too late; he passed on.

I believe, as my dad was lying there almost dead, his heart was thinking of me. The spiritual bond between us caused my spirit to feel his thoughts of me, and the Holy Spirit opened my eyes to see what was happening thousands of miles away from my location through vision.

God called him to rest. He served his purpose on Earth, and it was time to go to sleep until the resurrection morning; knowing this, I was okay with it. Every experience we encounter in this world is not strange; because the Bible warns us and prepares us even where injustice seems to prevail. Ecclesiastes 3:1, 2 says "to everything there is a season, a time for every purpose under heaven: a time to be born, and a time to die; …"

So long Papa; till we meet again.

Let's not quench the Holy Spirit. He's to teach us all things, and reveal all things to us. He is God in us, we must recognize that, and be aware of his functions in our lives; and all will be well with us.

CHAPTER SIX

Let's not quench the Holy Spirit. He's to teach us all things, and reveal all things to us. He is God in us, we must recognize that, and be aware of his functions in our lives; and all will be well with us.

Chapter Seven

THE BELIEF PRINCIPLE

Your Beliefs, not your circumstances, determine your peace and happiness.

The most important of my nuggets is the one I discovered during my tests and tribulations of life.

NUGGET 21:

Your beliefs, and not your circumstances, determine your peace and happiness; as I'll later explain in one of my testimonies.

The context of this book focuses on the belief principle; that is our belief in God, and how the belief system applies or operates in our daily living. To believe in God is to have confidence and trust in the Almighty—The Supreme Power.

The following testimonies will demonstrate how the belief system works:

Testimony One

WHEN YOUR HEART IS BITTER

Hold on to the Blessed Assurance

When your heart is bitter, turn to the Lord because He is the Master of peace.

In 2003, I was in Africa. One night I had a nightmare, I dreamt I saw a dead body covered with a white bed sheet, and that the person under the bed sheet was my child. When I woke up, sweat was running on my body as if I was placed on top of fire. It was a cool night, and the ceiling fan was blowing. The dream seemed and felt so real. I looked at the clock as my heart was panting, it was almost 6 A.M. our time. My first instinct was to pick up the phone and call my children. I dialed the phone repeatedly, but the network disappointed. Then I remembered that I spoke to my husband earlier—the previous evening for us while it was still the same day for my family in the U.S. A. Remembering this, was a little consolation for me; as I was still very much in despair.

Chapter Seven

Suddenly, I felt the urge to pray and, even though I was alone in my room, it seemed as if someone was telling me to pray the prayer of intervention, or intercessory prayer. Then, I realized before trying to make a call, prayer should have been the first thing I did. And I knelt beside my bed and cried to my God.

After the prayer, I looked at the time again, it was about 7 A.M., and I said to myself, "You must wait till at least their 5 A.M.", about another five hours. Meanwhile, I sent for one of my sisters, who was also my prayer partner at the time. When she arrived at my house, I told her about my nightmare. She tried convincing me that it was only a dream, and not to read too much out of it. But I knew better, my motherly God instinct convinced me otherwise.

"I know this is not just a dream," I said to her. As tears were gushing from my eyes, she looked at me and said, "Weeping will not solve the problem; if you feel the way you do, then now is the time to pray."

"We need to send our petition to God through an intercessory prayer," she added. I poured my heart to God in lamentation like I never prayed before in my life. Thank God for a prayer warrior sister and friend. I felt a little better afterwards.

Unfortunately, I had a scheduled assignment that would take me outside the state that day on behalf of a friend that needed my moral support. I picked up courage and went with the anticipation of excusing myself to return early. When we entered the other state we were visiting, I tried again.

After some hours of desperate attempts, the call went through when I almost gave up. The phone rang only once and I heard a panicky trembling little voice on the phone saying "Hello." It was as if the person was standing right there by the phone expecting it to ring. I said, "Who is on the phone?" The next thing I heard was, "Mommy, have you heard about Ronald?" "What about Ronald?" I said. "He had an accident. It's pretty bad, Mommy." And the line went dead. Throughout the journey, I kept on trying to reach my family on the phone, all to no avail. Needless to mention that fear and anxiety took away my joy the whole day. However, we returned home early as planned and I journeyed to the next city to a call center to call my family. It was almost closing time, I pleaded with the people to help me. We tried for about an hour and couldn't get through.

I went back home and spent a sleepless night. About the early morning hours, my husband called me, having heard I had called. He told me how the accident happened, but up to that moment he had not seen our son. I asked him, "What did the doctors say before they took him to the theatre for surgery. In a nutshell, he told me it was bad bad and that it was not looking good.

Several hours later, I succeeded in my phone call to my husband through the call center. He still didn't have any news for me.

However, while all this was going on, I did not stop praying for a miracle, for my son to be given another chance to live. During this incident, I prayed all types of prayers that the word of God speaks of without even realizing it at the time. Sometimes my heart would be so heavy that words would

Chapter Seven

cease in my mouth, then, I'd turn to the book of Psalms and meditate on the words of supplication until the Holy Spirit revived me to form my own words again in my quiet time with God.

For over fifty hours I lived with heartache and anticipation of hearing some good news about my son.

Finally, I found out that he'd survive, but not knowing if he would ever walk again devastated me. I became so bitter that instead of focusing on my preparation to returning to the United States, I focused on who to blame. In no time, I made myself the victim; I slipped into a temporary depression because I kept on blaming myself. I felt that if I did not travel, if I had been home, the accident wouldn't have happened. I gave myself several scenarios to justify my guilt, such as the boy worked long hours; he came back home late in the night. He did not get enough sleep, and a new teenage driver had been compelled to go out that early in a foggy weather.

If I were there first of all I would have been the one to drive out that early. Secondly, even if he wanted to, I wouldn't have allowed him. And the list went on and on. The more I thought about it, the more bitter I became.

One day, after I returned to the United States, I took my son to the hospital for a doctors' appointment. That day an x-ray of his broken leg was taken. While I was sitting in the waiting lounge, his orthopedic doctor sent for me. As I went in, my son's face illuminated with joy. He said, "Mom, I just want you to see this. My bones around the rod have started healing. And, did I tell you? Maybe I forgot to mention this to you, when I was in the hospital, I grew two inches." Tears came out of my eyes again only this time, they were tears of joy.

The day before his appointment, he had been very depressed. He had shared with me how he loves playing basketball, and now he could no longer play.

Although I was not strong emotionally myself, I tried to console him, asking him to focus first on being able to walk again. Before I went to bed that night, I went to a private corner to pray to God. I thanked Him for bringing my child back to life; I prayed that He would give me a testimony, another miracle, that my son should recover a hundred percent (100%). "Restore his legs to walk again, and I'll share the testimony of your goodness to the world."

I am sharing this testimony to help mothers or families that may be facing any type of crisis. In time of crisis, remember, the God when there is peace is the same God when we are going through crises. The important thing is that we must remain faithful to Him, and trust Him.

The evening after we came back from the hospital, before dinner, I went to my prayer corner and thanked God in prayer. This time I did not ask Him to heal my son; rather, I asked Him to heal my heartache, and to release me from the bondage of bitterness to be able to forgive myself. The following morning, something happened, I don't know how to accurately explain it even now. All I know is that I felt different and lighter. My heart was no longer heavy. My heart was filled with gratitude toward God. My whole context of the incident changed after that. Instead of focusing on blames and why, I started viewing the whole situation with a different light. Moreover, my heart was filled with gratitude to God for giving my son another chance to live, and to fulfill his purpose on earth. I had an inner peace in my heart that gave me hope. And all my supplications to God convinced and convicted me, that my son would walk again.

Even though my son's physical condition had not changed, I kept on thanking God for what He has done for me and my family. For giving us the opportunity to get closer to Him, and have a more unified love for one another. I thanked God for what He already did, and for what I was still expecting Him to do. I'd say "Thank You, Lord, for healing my son a hundred percent. And I thank You that I see my son walking again." My son's healing improved week after week, month after month until he became one hundred percent whole again. I thank God, every day for His goodness.

Testimony Two

THE ESSENCE OF MEMORY

Why do we forget God's faithfulness easily?

On Valentine's Day *February 14, 1992* a tragedy occurred in my family. And during this tragedy, God gave me and my family the greatest miracle in our lives.

In this joyful valentine's day afternoon, I put my baby to sleep and laid her on her crib, and left the apartment to go and pick up my oldest daughter from her elementary school, who had stayed for an after-school activity. In less than forty minutes when I returned, I was no longer allowed to drive into my apartment complex. Closing of the apartment complex driveway left a long traffic jam on Austell road. I eagerly wanted to see what was going on, so I squeezed onto the curb and I saw that the driveway was blocked by firemen and police. As I noticed several fire trucks and police cars at the scene, in an instant, I had this strong feeling it was my building. I parked the car right there on the road and asked my daughter to wait inside the car. Instantly, I changed my mind and took her with me. I ran inside the taped area and some of the fire and policemen shouted woman you can't go in there. I ignored them and kept on running and yelling "my children are in there; my children are in that building". Little

Chapter Seven

did I know that the fire wasn't just in my building but in my apartment. In a matter of seconds, I noticed the fire on the roof of my apartment. At that moment, I felt like my world has just ended. As I was running towards the burning building two men were running after me, and one of them grabbed my daughter while the other tried to restrain me and said to me "it's dangerous you can't go inside." In the Panic of shouting, "my children, my children," I tried to let myself loose from the man. A neighbor shouted, "your children are safe."

Hearing the word 'safe' I experienced what seemed like a lump of peace hit on my racing heart with a force. I don't have the right description for what I felt; perhaps relief is an understatement. The neighbor led me to where my nine-year-old was receiving first aid treatment near the ambulance for smoke inhalation. I also saw my house guest with her infant, the lady who was taking care of my children when the incident happened. I asked her for my other three kids, and she pointed to a building at the back telling me a man took them that way. The building she pointed at was where my kids' babysitter lived, naturally I went to her apartment first to look for my kids. And there they were; the youngest was seven months old.

Then I discovered I almost lost two children in that fire. The fire started in the bedroom where my nine-year-old was doing his school project and he used some clean laundry in a laundry basket that was on the bed to put off the fire and flame escalated. Our house guest in a panic ran out with three little kids with her in the living room. A Good Samaritan named Ron who was also the husband of my kids' babysitter saved my children from the burning apartment. What happened was a miracle. As a matter of fact, Ron the

'Good Samaritan' usually was at work during that period, but something happened and he came home early. He had walked out to go and buy something at the neighborhood convenient store when he noticed the smoke on the roof, he ran towards the building suspecting it was my apartment.

He heard a woman shouting, "two children are inside". He inquired of the kids' location and he ran in before the firefighters arrived. According to him, the moment he picked up the baby from her crib, the ceiling collapsed on the crib. Also, coming out of the bedroom, fire from the fourth bedroom was already penetrating the hallway because he broke the door open to save my nine-year-old first before going for the baby. My son had locked the door to stop the fire on his own, but by the time he realized that stopping the fire was beyond his ability, he could no longer see the doorknob to open the door. He was blinded by the smoke; hence, he fell on the floor practicing the fire drill he learned in school. I believe his fire drill experience bought him some time to survive the fire.

It was truly a miracle that God saved my two children from that hostile fire that burned down the apartment in a matter of minutes. We lost every property we owned. All we had were the clothes on our bodies. By the time my husband returned from work, our home was gone.

Despite the tragedy, that day remained one of the most memorable and joyous days of our lives. In fact, I still cannot imagine my life and that of the rest of my family members if we had lost the two kids that day. It obviously would have made a negative impact in our lives. In addition to the miracle, God supplied us with our basic needs through the help of our Church members in Marietta Seventh-Day Adventist Church,

Chapter Seven

in Georgia; my children's School, the Red Cross, some friends, and relatives. Without this help, life would have been much tougher, because we had no form of property insurance.

In my previous testimony, when I snapped out of my bitterness, I remembered the fire incident and the miracle God gave us that day. I felt sad and disappointed in myself that I had forgotten God's faithfulness in our lives over the years. I prayed, that God forgive me and help me to always look at the Cross, no matter the crises I may encounter; because the Grace of my Lord is sufficient for me.

And for you reading this book, I hope you never forget to always count your blessings no matter what. Although our circumstances may sometimes bring us down, but it is important not to forget that God is always present, and ready to see us through our life struggles.

Talking about God's presence in our situations: in the fire incident, even though we lost all our household properties and clothing in that fire, besides the miracle of the survival of our two children, we were favored with another miracle we could not explain. Most of our important documents survived without a fireproof safe, we had none at the time. The files and the envelopes we saved them in were not destroyed by the fire, nor by the water used to hose down the fire. Only God has the answer.

Testimony Three

A TURNING POINT

"With God, all things are possible"

The story I'm about to share with you is to demonstrate one of the benefits you will achieve as a parent when you become a good shepherd to your children by leading them to the Chief Shepherd, our Lord and Savior Jesus Christ.

For years I prayed with my children for just about everything. Especially, one of my daughters made it a habit, she'd call me or come to me and say, "Mom, let's pray for this or that." It happened during her college years; she got the opportunity to travel to Europe a couple of times from six weeks to six months on study abroad programs. No matter where she was, whether in the United States or in Europe, she'd call me for us to pray for different things. From her studies, writing of exams to finding an apartment or getting a nice dorm room in her school.

After high school, her father and I tried convincing her to go to school in our home state due to financial reasons. One day, I sat her down and tried to explain to her to understand why we want her to go to school at home where she would pay in-state tuition. And that if she stayed within our state, her scholarship money would cover everything. But if she goes outside the state the money would cover less than fifty percent of her school expenses. She replied, "Mom, I appreciate your concern. I'll just say two things to you. First of all, I did not work so hard to be an honor student so I could go to just any University. Second of all, have you forgotten what you have been teaching me from when I was a little kid?" "What is that?" I asked. "You told me to trust in God. And you said if I asked God for anything, I should have faith, believing that God will endorse it, and that's what I have done. I know it in my heart that God will provide for me, I just know it," she added. Well then, I said, "May the Lord answer all your prayers in Jesus' name." "Amen," we both confirmed.

I told my husband to please allow her to go to the university where her heart was. He said with sarcasm, "I hope she knows how she'd get the remaining money, because I just can't handle it now." In my mind, I had a joyful response; I said the "All" will take care of that. Our praying together continued and she won more scholarship awards and other financial aid assistance.

My major turning point in my spiritual life:

One day my daughter called me; she had a desperate situation. She was in a foreign land for the first time without a family member, and she needed an apartment because the arrangement that was made for her while she was still in the United States had failed. During this period, a severe storm was raging in my life, and I was spiritually down. And when she told me her problem, I was worried for her—a teenage girl in a foreign land with no place to stay. She said, "Mom, I found one and I desperately need to get that apartment, apartments are difficult here to find. So, let's pray that I get it," she said. "I'll pray for you tonight," I said. "That's fine, but can we pray now? Pray with me over the phone," she insisted.

"Okay!" I closed my office door, because I was at work, and I prayed with her.

I was spiritually very down that day. I felt I was not in the mood for prayer, so my prayer went like this: first, I thanked God for His favor upon my daughter. Second, I said to God, "This child believes in You and has the confidence that whatever requests she sends your way, that you always fulfill her heart desires. I pray that you do the same for her now according to her faith." Third, I prayed that God's Will be done in her life; and finally, I thanked God for answering our prayers in Jesus our Savior's name we pray. Amen. We both confirmed. After the prayers I said to her, "May God guide and protect you." After all these happened, I took a reality check of my life. I thought about all the storms and earthquakes in my life at the time.

Later that evening at home, I repeated the prayer and asked God not to disappoint her; to answer her positively not because of my faith, but because of her own faith and belief in Him.

I directed the prayer towards my daughter's faith because I felt my faith could not save the situation at that time. I had allowed the devil to handicap my faith due to the storm I was going through.

The very next day she called me with all excitement. "Mom, I have good news for you." "That's great," I said. "Tell me, tell me, did you get the apartment?" "No. God answered our prayers speedily, with no delay at all." "I'm confused, but you just said you didn't get the place." "Yes, I didn't get it," she said. I was like okay, waiting anxiously to hear the good news and it seemed to me like she was not talking fast enough. First, she told me how happy she was that she didn't get the place and why? "But where are you going to stay?" I interjected. "Mom, wait," she responded, "God gave me something a whole lot better." Her explanation included a young lady as her roommate with a car who had promised to give her ride to work and show her places. In summary, she found a friend who was like a sister to her with the apartment. And after speaking to the young lady myself later, my heart was settled as far as my concern of my baby being out there by herself.

The devil sending storms to pull my feet off the ground, and earthquakes so the ground would swallow me. And I got really mad at the devil, and I verbally said to him, "You are finished." My Savior already paid my debt in full, I owe you nothing. You have no hold on me. I am not afraid of you, my God is with me, I am for Jesus forever. I know God gave me this assignment, and you have no say in it. Be gone. And never ever dare come to torture me again. I'm not your instrument, and I do not belong in your council. You devil depart from me, you and your agents. Don't dare cross my way; I am an anointed of God."

"My God has sent me here for a purpose and I must fulfill the will of God whether you like it or not."

In addition to my verbal rebuke of the devil, for several nights I prayed like an angry lion, rebuking the devil to leave me and my family alone. I pledged the blood of Jesus; I still do, and I will continue pledging my Savior's blood till the end of time.

I was liberated by my daughter's faith. I got up and started writing a drama for the youth I was serving which included, Philippians 4:13 which says, "I can do all things through Christ who strengthens me." And how God is never in a hurry, yet He's always on time. "With God, everything is possible."

Brothers and sisters, God's time is always the best. And when we believe and trust in the Lord, miracles happen, because He's still in the miracle business.

CHAPTER SEVEN

Testimony Four

A MOTHER'S PRAYER

Have faith and trust in the Lord

In early May of 2009, after dinner I refreshed and picked up a book to read before bedtime. As I was reading, in a trance, I saw my youngest child weeping. I got up immediately and wondered if my mind was playing a trick on me. I said to myself, it must be my feeling of missing my family; or perhaps I have been thinking about her and her school activities lately.

Well, to put my mind at peace, I picked up the phone and called her. And behold, she was crying. I asked her what the matter was repeatedly but I couldn't get an answer from her. I specifically asked if her father was okay, she said yes. I asked several specific questions about everyone in our family and nothing was wrong. "Then why are you so hysterical if all is well." "All is not well," she said. "Then tell me, what is it?"

My kids normally share everything with me, what is wrong this time that she cannot tell me? So, I insisted to know what was going on, but my effort did not yield any fruit. All she said was, "Mom, it's just my problem, you don't need to worry about it." And I responded, "your problem is my problem why can't you allow me in to help you?"

And then she said, "you're over there, there's nothing you can do for me. You don't need to worry, Mom."

Even though she was right, but her response hurt; and my heart was broken because I couldn't do anything to help my child. I wasn't there to put my arms around her. At the end I said to her, "Sweetheart, you know I love you, but there's someone who loves you even more, and can do better at solving problems way more than I can, even if I'm there with you, no matter what it is." I continued by telling her to stop crying and talk to God. "What you need to do now is stop crying and talk to God; He's always willing to listen and He knows your pain right now." In addition, I said "even if He knows your problem, open your mouth and tell Him and ask Him to take care of it for you, because He can change any situation in a second. I know He will do it, just ask Him."

She sobered and said, "Okay Mommy, I love you," and I said, "I love you too." On my path, I prayed and sent my humble and honest petition to God, and I said my geographical position does not matter, I cannot do anything on my own to stop her from hurting, rather, He's the only one who can. "Please Father, help me console and take care of my child." I also pleaded with God to send an angel to hug my daughter for me. At least I could have done that if I were there with her.

The next day I called her, and she was all upbeat in her normal cheerful voice. "I guess you're alright now?" "Yes," she responded. I further asked, "is the situation taken care of now?" "You said God will take care of everything, I'll leave it at that," she replied. "That's right," I said.

A few weeks later, I returned to the United States for her

high school graduation. I decided I'd not get into the situation until after her graduation day.

As the overwhelming cheer of the crowd vibrates the graduation arena, and the noise sounding like a thundering storm as my daughter's name was called as the Valedictorian of the class of 2009, I immediately had a strong impression in my heart, that what was happening then must be a contributing factor to her worries previously. After the graduation date, we received a letter from the Governor of our state, an invitation to a reception at the Governor's mansion in the honor of my daughter Stephanie for her excellent academic achievement. Now, when we were sharing the excitement, I asked her what really happened. In summary, I found out her counselor submitted some of her grades late after the deadline. And she was afraid that error could cause her all her hard work over the years in her high school education.

The truth is that if I were within the country, nothing or nobody could have been able to stop me from going to that school to confront the individuals concerned. Thank God for He is always able to salvage, restructure, and restore whatever is broken in our lives, He makes it anew. Hallelujah!

When the storms of life are raging,
Keep pressing on.
Never be discouraged;
Have faith and trust in the Lord.

Chapter Eight

PUTTING BELIEF TO WORK!

Belief is a choice

Your belief can result to a negative or positive reaction depending on your context of the content of your situation(s).

In other words, belief is a result of some natural factors that are embedded over time, to our subconscious self which influences our inner self and reflects in our behavior— the way we see things.

In order for belief to work positively for us, we must have an insight, a clear understanding of our feelings, of our inner self. And we must separate our inner emotion from our circumstance(s), to make sure that our circumstance does not dictate our action. Having an insight of your inner self will help you to identify with the reality of your situation, and the way you view it.

For example, let me explain my context of the contents of the situations in my testimonies. In my first testimony, my bitterness clouded my judgment. I focused on my hurt. All I could see in that situation was the bad thing that happened to me. My context led me to looking for someone to blame, and dwelling on the ifs and whys. I saw nothing positive from that situation; especially, while I was watching my son suffering in pain. When I opened the trunk of my car and saw the white bed sheet with blood that reminded me his car was no more. And when I was called by the doctor to see the x-ray, and I centered my attention on the rod inside his body and I was overwhelmed with pity and scared, instead of seeing the bone healing. Not until I realized that my son smiled for the first time in months; I saw nothing good in my interpretation of the context of that situation.

But when my heart was renewed, it was like a ray of light touched my inner self, and my understanding of the context of that same situation changed. My perception changed drastically. Instead of blame and regret, I had gratitude and appreciation. After the special prayers, I could get in touch with my inner self and understand how I was allowing the situation to influence me negatively.

Understanding this, helped me to reverse my feeling about the situation and I could face the reality of the current event. Yes, the accident was real, it happened. But how do we survive beyond that? As my perception changed positively, I could then focus on my son being well again. I was grateful to God that He spared his life. I was more appreciative of the Good Samaritan that called 911 (emergency call for medical ambulance); perhaps a minute later the boy probably wouldn't have been alive. I appreciated the health personnel that put in their best to make sure the boy survived. I appreciated other members of my family that did their best to make the situation more manageable, and their help to their brother, son, and cousin. Most importantly, I appreciated God for His promise that He would not allow me to go through a test I could not handle. In addition, I cherish God for giving me the gift of dream; the opportunity of seeing what was to happen and His answer to our prayers.

Furthermore, for my tribulations and the storms in Africa, I started seeing every situation I thought was bad in a different light. A sudden understanding came to me that God was allowing me to go through that experience to fortify me and ground me for something bigger. The devil intensifies his efforts when he notices that God is about to reposition you to a higher platform. Instead of grumbling and complaining, I expressed my gratitude to God in praises and prayers for trusting someone like me with an assignment of such magnitude; even though I still don't understand everything. I feel blessed and favored by His love for me. In return, I ask Him daily to give me patience and wisdom in all my endeavors.

In summary, when we make Christ the center of our lives, we stay in God's plan, and everything else will fall into place according to His will.

All good things come from God: While the devil is busy working overtime to deposit fear, troubles, and intimidation in our lives. If Christ is the center of our lives, God will liberate us spiritually above all our enemies' plots. He'll wrap us in a holy foundation that will never collapse. Hallelujah!

Chapter Nine

THE POWER OF PRAYER

Prayer is a response to God's call

As I earlier stated, **"a life without a purpose or direction is not worth living."** But how do you identify your God-given purpose on Earth? You can discover your purpose on Earth through obedience to God. And to obey God, you must be able to hear him. It would be difficult to obey if you cannot identify the voice of God in your heart.

To hear God, you must first know Him. Second, you must be close to Him. Third, you must be dependent on Him, by trusting His Will. And finally, you must obey Him as He leads your way.

The first step to achieving the aforementioned characteristics is through prayer. In prayer, we adore and praise our God; in prayer, we confess our sins, send our petitions or supplications to God. And in prayer, we show our gratitude to God through thanksgiving.

WHAT IS PRAYER?

First of all, the word pray, according to Oxford Advanced Learner's Dictionary means "to speak to God, especially to give thanks or ask for help: And prayer are words which you say to God giving thanks or asking for help." In Webster's dictionary: Pray is "to ask earnestly: Beg (2) To address God with adoration, pleading, or thanksgiving. In the other words, Prayer is a request addressed to God:' (2) "The act of praying to God:(3) A set form of words used in praying: (4) A religious service that is mostly prayers."

Therefore, I would like to define prayer as the spiritual thirst or quest for God's love, surrendering our heart desires to the Supreme Power of the Almighty, knowing that we cannot change our circumstances without Him.

We thirst for God's love by recognizing that He's seeking for us, and we need to connect with Him. Furthermore, we surrender our heart desires, what our minds focuses on, to God when we faithfully believe that He's the only way to life and freedom through our Lord Jesus Christ. In a nutshell, **prayer is a response to God's call—** for He made Himself available to us first.

I have a separate book written about prayer, which will be published following this book. Therefore, what I have presented here is a brief discussion on "The Power of Prayer".

Chapter Nine

In my prayer book, you'll find out in detail— the WWWH of prayer— Why we pray? What happens when we pray? When do we pray? And How to pray. Also, you will discover the twenty benefits of prayer, types of prayer and more.

Prayer is a Prescribed Master Key to All Doors of Achievement and Success.

Chapter Ten

TESTIMONY FIVE
INTERCESSORY PRAYER
IN ACTION

Don't pray just for yourselves, pray for one another

The night of March 17, 2011 is a night I will never forget as long as I live. The night God gave me another miracle of life. About 1 A.M, my husband and I heard voices within our compound. In no time, we heard a very soldier-like voice interrogating our driver, bombarding him with questions about the owner of the house, and asking him to open the corridor gate. The driver with trembling voice, persistently responded, "I don't have the key." He was knelt down, pushed and beaten to open the protector, but he kept on saying, "please I don't have the key; don't hit me!"

We had just buried my stepmother that very day. The whole week, we had been running around in preparation for the burial ceremony. After the burial, we were very exhausted and needed to at least get some sleep that night. We got home and there was no electricity. We had left our generator in the village for our guests. We only went home to have some sleep after being up for two nights.

However, the moon was shining very bright outside. At the sound of the noise, I went into my living room from my bedroom and I saw two men in army uniforms and two others. The men in army uniforms had long guns with them. I went back to my bedroom and whispered to my husband what I saw. Before I went back to my bedroom, I saw one of the other men pick up a Saw and gave one of the uniformed men and he started sawing the protector. In a panic, there was a noise in our room when we were trying to reach a phone in the dark, because we couldn't use the flashlight to avoid alerting them of our position. Then, we heard more voices from the backyard, they started yelling out at us to come out and let them in. When we did not respond, they started breaking our bedroom and toilet window glasses, threatening to shoot us through the windows.

By this time, we realized they were armed robbers and we relocated within the house. After about an hour of trying without success, they became more violent in smashing of windows and intensified their efforts to cut the padlocks and the protectors. Suddenly, I heard a boot hit, at the door, where my husband was, and it opened. I heard the rage in their voices because we would not let them in. I had no choice but to open the door of the living room; I didn't want them to hurt or kill my husband. And this was the beginning of our nightmare.

Chapter Ten

First, they began by collecting all our cell phones and laptops. They collected every dime they found and at the same time, compelled us to give them all the money we had. After much interrogation and looting, one of them said if we give them one million Naira they would go. I kept telling them we had no million Naira; besides who keeps such an amount of money at home? Then the wicked Robber said, "then we will take you to our camp until your husband brings the money, you will not be released." I said to him, "I'm not going to any camp with you." "Go and get dressed he shouted at me." "It's dark I can't see," I replied. The second Robber said "okay, take my torch," which was our own flashlight. Before I could stretch my hand to collect it, the wicked Robber snatched it from him and queried him, "what are you are doing?" He flashed light in my closet and ordered me to go get my clothes, and I refused. "If you're taking me to camp you have to take me like this, the way I am now," I stood my ground.

"Even if you take me, my husband does not have that money to give you." He cocked his gun and said, "I will kill you now." The other one said to him, "don't shoot her." And at the same time, he turned to me and said, "go bring any amount you have and we will leave you." I continued telling them I had no other money, even what they collected was not all our money, which was the truth. But my answer was not satisfactory to them. He ordered his colleague to take me to their group outside, and that he was coming. At this point I said to myself what if he kills my husband. In a moment, I heard myself saying, "can I give you people a check for the one million?" I said this even though I knew I had no such money. "We don't take checks" he replied. At the same time, my husband shouted; "bring my inhaler, bring my inhaler." They didn't allow me to go look for it. In an instant, I heard myself preaching to them. "Look! You are children of God, please have mercy!" I continued, "if you repent now and accept Jesus, He will forgive you. Still take everything you have already taken from us. Just save yourselves, don't commit murder."

The good robber then asked me, "where is the inhaler? What is it?" I told them he was having problem breathing that he could die. I said please don't allow his blood to be on your head. Then he said, "go and get the inhaler." Soon after I gave my husband the inhaler, the wicked robber ordered me at gunpoint to cross the courtyard and open the second parlor, the guest suite, and all the other rooms in the courtyard.

After opening all the doors except one, my home office, he shouted at me to hurry and open that too. I told him the key was not on that bunch of keys. Fortunately, the window was open and the window cotton was slanted to one side. As he kept insisting, I should open that door too, I told him to look through the window. It's an office with a bunch of books," I said. Then he ushered me back to the guest suite area, he asked me to enter the bathtub in the bathroom and face the wall. I asked him why? He became very furious and called me "stubborn woman, do you know this is a real gun and shouted at me to go inside the bathtub facing the wall. It seemed I heard a voice saying, "don't; he'd kill you." Therefore, I turned and walked straight to the main living room where my husband was. In my mind, I said if anything is to happen at least let me be with my husband. I had no fear of death; my heart was as solid as a rock.

As I was about entering the veranda of my living room, I felt a sharp sudden pain on my left shoulder from the head of his

Chapter Ten

gun. I screamed ah… but I didn't turn my head, I continued walking straight to where my husband was and I sat on a chair. My action ignited a flame of fire in his anger and the situation became worse. While he was communicating with the other one in uniform, I found out he was their ringleader. He joined the other one ransacking every corner of the house again as if they were the owners of the house.

What they were doing to our properties was tearing my heart; so, I asked, what are you looking for? The one that wanted to shoot me said, "Shut up. When I see it, I will know." And he kept moving from one corner of the house to another like a chicken without a head. He said to the other one he was going back to check the other side and he zoomed out.

After a while, he called the other one with us out to the front door of our living room. They left together to the side of the building—our parking lot. Before he left, he told us not to move an inch; if we didn't want trouble. After a while, the second robber came back, stopped at the door and called me, "Madam, come and lock your door." As I approached the door, he threw a bunch of keys to me and repeated lock your gate. I was very numb at this point. I picked the bunch of keys from the floor before I could get up, one from his group gave him something but I didn't see his face, and he turned back and handed another bunch of keys to me and said, "here is your jeep key." The only thing that came out of my mouth was "God bless you." Why in the world would I bless an armed robber who had just robbed and tormented me mentally, emotionally and physically without pity? I didn't get it.

After they left, I called my driver whom they left with bruises, because he did not open the protector for them. All of us went around the compound to solve the puzzle of how they came in without coming in through the protector gates and doors. We finally discovered they came with a ladder, climbed over the roof and into the courtyard. After they made their way in, they broke the padlock on the back-metal door. Inside our Toyota 4Runner, which they called jeep, was our video camera and picture camera was on the dining table; they took all. All the memories of my stepmother's burial and other important family memorable activities were gone with the cameras.

Though they collected a lot of tangible items such as money and properties, but the intangible items hurt me the most, because they cannot be replaced. And they would mean nothing to them nor be of any use to them.

These armed robbers arrived our premises about 1 A.M. and did not leave until after 5 A.M. The agony of their torment felt like they were there much longer than the four hours. After going round, the four of us which included our guest sat in the courtyard agonizing over the whole situation. Then I said we have a lot to be thankful for. Our guest concurred and said, "especially for our lives." He added that he couldn't believe my boldness challenging a man who was pointing a gun at me, knowing that pity was not in his heart. I asked him, how he heard my conversation with him, because when the armed robber forced me to open his room he noticed someone was in the room, but didn't see anyone. He asked me "who was there?" I said this is our guest suite but didn't tell him someone was there that night. Then our guest responded, "I heard all your discussions from where I was hiding."

Chapter Ten

My husband said "yea, we need to thank God." He continued that the first thing he checked after they left, were his traveling documents, passports and ticket and they were intact. Even though they ransacked over where he put them, they did not notice them.

At this point, we decided to call some relatives and friends, and shared our horrible experience. At daybreak, people started visiting to sympathize with us and were telling me how lucky we were, especially myself who was challenging that wicked robber with gun. Among all the visitors that came that Friday and the next few days, what was said by two visitors among them who came at different times and didn't know each other stood out in my mind: First, was one of our family friends who said, he believed that prayers of those orphans I was training prevented me from being killed that night. Second, was my village church pastor, who came to the house to pray with us after the weekend; by this time, we already heard the terrible news—a businessman being killed by the same group of armed robbers that came to our house.

They came to our house on Thursday night. On Saturday night, two days later, they went to this businessman's family. They did not only take his money, they took his life also. According to the story, after they short him to death, they threw some money at the wife to use and bury the husband whom they just murdered.

What did my Pastor say? He was overwhelmed and speechless for a while after my husband and I narrated our ordeal to him, because he missed our testimony in the church. First, he thanked God for everything and for the preservation of our lives. In addition, he said, "sister Fyne you are truly blessed."

He believed there was a supernatural intervention. He said, "I believe the Angels of God were praying for you." At this point, my Pastor was not aware of the other man's robbery and killing. I told him after what he said to me.

After my pastor left, I revisited the incident of that night in my memory. Then it hit me! Our survival was not ordinary; there was a supernatural involvement. Bit by bit, I analyzed the occurrence of that night.

Normally, we leave the hallway gate key to the security or whoever sleeps in the security room. That night, because the security was not there, I asked the driver to sleep in the security room so he could answer to knocks at the gate in the morning, since we were all very tired. After we had gone to bed, I went back out to my front veranda about 11 PM and requested to have the key back. Secondly, after I heard my husband's voice and I decided to open the parlor door because I knew they got him. He was asked to lay on the floor while already his hands were up. As he was obeying them, the crazy one among them hit him with his boot; and I challenged him to stop it, and that he should have a little respect for his elder. He poured me dirty water and hit me on my head with a frying pan.

As they were scattering and tossing our bedroom and walk-in closet upside down, and after collecting all the money with us, both the money they found themselves and the money we gave them, they still asked us for more money, and I said they have collected all we had. Then one of them said "what about the dollars your husband brought from the U.S.A.," I responded; "my husband has been home for some weeks now and we just buried my stepmother today", I picked one of the

Chapter Ten

burial brochures and showed them. Of course, it made no difference to them.

Also, I remembered when he was ushering me to enter not only the bathroom, but the bathtub and face the wall, and the Holy Spirit spoke to me. For a second time, I preached to him again. I said to him, "young man, God has a purpose for you on earth, don't miss it. It's not late for you to tell God I'm sorry. He will forgive you and still help you to achieve what he brought you here on earth for." He snapped at me and said, "don't you tell me anything about God anymore". That was when he said to me, "do you know that this gun is loaded? One more word from you, I will shoot. You worship God, I worship Satan," he added. After this exchange of words, was when I decided to go to where my husband was in the parlor. Before my first step I looked at him and said, "I know my God have sent me to planet earth for a good purpose. If my God feels I have already fulfilled my assignment here on earth, well so be it; but if I have not concluded my assignment on earth, you will not shoot me." Then, I turned and walked away. To explain to you how hard the blow of the gun head was on my shoulder, the pain, even with medication, lasted for over six months.

The most amazing thing in this story is the fact that I had no atom of fear in me throughout the ordeal, regardless of their threats.

All my actions that night was out of my character, especially blessing a robber who had put me through hell; not to mention the wrong timing in preaching the word of God. After my analysis, I felt like someone else was in me acting on my behalf. At that very moment, I didn't understand it. I just didn't get it.

About a week later, my husband went back to the United States of America. Five weeks later, I too returned to the U.S.A. for the summer. The first day I visited my church in Douglasville, Georgia in the U.S., after church, as I was greeting and chatting with people I had not seen for almost two years, when our pianist greeted with a hand wave I told my children let me go and say hello to her, and one of my daughters said, "oh, me too; I haven't seen her in a while." We both went. After we greeted, she said, Fyne, guess what? "We prayed for you." "Really!" I responded excitedly. And she turned to my daughter and said you too Jessica.

My excitement was because I've been gone for almost two years no communication with any member or the new pastor up to then; yet, they remembered to pray for me. A day selected for the whole church to pray for me. I'm not talking about prayer during church service; rather, a prayer dedicated just for me.

Out of curiosity, I asked her if she didn't mind, did she remember when it happened, like this year or last year? Then our pastor came to inquire of something of her, and she said, "Fyne, if you can wait a moment, I'll check for you." Of course, I opted to wait. I sent my daughter to go and tell my other kids to go home and leave one car for us.

When our pianist finished with the pastor, she called us closer and pulled a book and checked my prayer day was five days before the armed robbery occurred. And my daughter's own was the following month. The same time she needed the prayer desperately too. I know because within that period, she had called me while I was in Nigeria for a prayer request about something concerning her school. I asked my daughter whether she sent her request to the church too. She said no,

Chapter Ten

that she had not even been to our home church for about a year because of her school outside the state. I was overcome by the love of God for me and my family.

We had a scheduled visitation after church, but I was overtaken with joy and I couldn't stop praising God. I just decided to go home straight. And as soon as I got home, I called my pastor in Nigeria, the one that visited us after the robbery. I said, Pastor Nteija, I have the most wonderful news to share with you from church I expressed with great excitement. He anxiously listened to hear the good news. "Do you remember what you told me when you visited us after the armed robbery?" "Remind me," he said. And I reminded him that he said, he believed angels of God were praying for me. "You were right," I said. In addition, I said both angels and saints of God were praying for me, as I shared with him what I found out.

I had wanted to share my testimony to the church that 2011 summer, but unfortunately, my activities took me to other states of U.S.A., and the opportunity eluded me.

When I came back in 2012 summer, the last Sabbath I worshiped with them before returning to Nigeria, I told my Pastor and two of our elders I had a testimony I needed to share with the church since last summer, and that day was my last worship with them for the summer. I was given an opportunity to tell my story by testifying the amazing grace of our Lord upon our lives, how God saved our lives during an unusual circumstance. My story included how our pianist told me about their special prayers for me and I expressed my gratitude to them for their prayers. I encouraged the congregation that we need to keep on praying for one another, because our God answers prayers.

The wonderful thing about this testimony to the church was the fact that our pianist was there to hear when I said to the church that I did not tell her why I wanted to know the when of the prayer. Also, that she was hearing the story for the first time just like the rest of the church.

Furthermore, the reality of the whole ordeal finally sank into my emotion as I saw the empathizing eyes of the whole congregation glued on me as they listened as I narrated my experience during the armed robbery. I finally broke into tears, knowing that I did not deserve the grace of God; if not for Jesus, and the level of God's love for me. I could not comprehend it. My consolation is, knowing that Jesus finished all on the cross so I could be free and deserving of my heavenly Father's love.

All I need to know and understand is that my God works in a mysterious way. And I always will remain in His presence. Jesus' blood has set me free and I am saved. Glory be to our God, for his mercy endures forever.

Chapter Eleven

TESTIMONY SIX
THE DEVIL'S MIDNIGHT VISIT

"No weapon fashioned against you shall prosper."

On the night of July 9, 2008, just about the midnight hour, the unimaginable occurred. The enemy plotted a devilish spiritual execution attack against me. Thank God that I'm still here to tell the story.

Before this time, ever since I made my presence known in the place I called home, the agents of Satan had relentlessly devised all possible means to fight me spiritually in order not only to disable my voice, but to remove me from the stage so the children of the world would not hear the messages God has given me to deliver to them. Thank God! He who is in me is greater than he who is in the world.

On the above-mentioned date, my day was filled with activities which was not unusual at that time of the year;

ranging from preparation for final examination to setting the stage for graduation. I got home about 7 P.M. After my home routine, I found myself in my home office, writing an address, a speech for the graduation ceremony. By 10 P.M, I was ready to retire, and I left for my bedroom to start my devotion routine. After which, I realized that sleep was far from my eyes, so I decided to work on my bed. I had recently at the time written a new anthem for the school which the students had not mastered yet.

The anthem was to be used on the graduation ceremony, which was in about a week. With the students still focusing on their final exams, a thought came to my mind, I decided to record the anthem to make it easier for the music teacher to teach the children and orchestrate it with the band. As I finished recording, I got caught up in the mood of praising and worshiping the Lord until about midnight. I closed by reading a passage from Psalms. Then I got up to turn on the walk-in closet light then switched off the bedroom light.

I fluffed my pillows, and laid down. Almost immediately, I saw a very tall, huge image, the body from head to toe was covered with white native chalk, the eyes color was like a mixture of red and fire. I'm calling it image because, though it looked like a man and it was there in the flesh, but it was not a human being. The chalk covered even the lips. He had things on his hands I couldn't tell what, because my eyes focused on what was drawn on his chest, a heart in red with a black line crossing the heart. I sat up quickly simultaneously the following questions popped out: Who are you? What are you doing here? How did you get in here? The meanness on his face I had never seen in my life. By this time, I knew it was the devil himself.

Chapter Eleven

As I was talking to him, my right hand was behind me looking for the Bible I just used and placed next to my other pillow; it wasn't there. I tried to reach the cell phone next to the Bible; it wasn't there. This thing was staring at me with a lot of anger on his face. Suddenly, I heard myself binding him—the devil. I said, "go back to wherever you came from. I have no business with you. I do not belong in your camp; you shouldn't be here." The thing did not bulge. I finally screamed "Jesus! I belong to Jesus; Jesus, Jesus my Savior, Jesus my Savior; help me Lord…" As I was chanting Jesus, praying loud, he started stepping backwards slowly as if he was moon walking. In an instant, he was sucked backwards, between the back window and the wall next to it. As this happened, the curtain did not shake, and the window was still locked.

I got up, switched on my light, sat back on the bed, I discovered both my Bible and my cell phone were intact right where I had placed them. But they weren't there earlier when I tried to reach them with my hand. I tried to comprehend what just happened, but I could not come up with any logical explanation for what I just experienced. I knew for sure that I was not sleeping, because when I decided to lay down, I was not sleepy yet; I only wanted to lay down until my body was ready to sleep after the praise and worship and singing. Also, the windows were all closed with burglary proof, with rods on the frames and protectors on the wall. Moreover, I knew it was not a human being and the image was there physically in the room.

As the analysis of what just happened went on in my head, something started growing inside of me. I don't have a name for it, but I can describe it as a mixture of gratitude, confidence, and anger. In my analysis, I laid out the following questions:

What if I was asleep at that hour, what would have happened to me? What if I never prayed that evening? What if God did not take away fear from me? Perhaps, such could lead to a heart attack, because I have heard of people that were found dead in the morning presumed to die in their sleep. What about when I tried to call Jesus and my jaws went stiffened. If the Holy Spirit hadn't helped me to call the word Jesus out after praying a prayer of heart. By this I mean when I could not pronounce Jesus, I called on God to help me first in my heart. The devil couldn't hear what I did not say aloud.

When I came to the reality of knowing that my life could have ended that night, an anger grew inside of me, as I was pouring out my gratitude to God for saving my life. It wasn't long confidence echoed in for there was no atom of fear inside of me during and after the ordeal. Therefore, I decided for that very night, no more sleep. I put on my Armor of God, I took my shield and sword for war against the enemy. But I knew I could not fight the battle on my own, so I invited my Lord who had just saved me again. I invited Him not as a lamb, but as a lion of Judah to roar against my enemies. Needless to say that, I turned the night to a night of warfare prayer.

While in prayer, the Lord opened my eyes in a vision; I saw that image that came to my bedroom. I saw him running. And that was when I saw what was in his hands. On one hand was a thick bag tied in the middle with rope with things inside, but I didn't see what was inside it. And on the other hand, he had a bow and an arrow. He was running back to where he began his journey.

Chapter Eleven

After this night, the nagging 'why' lingered in my mind with no simple answers. However, one thing is certain; God's assurance is for sure. He is always on my side; not by my side, for He lives inside of me.

Chapter Twelve

TESTIMONY SEVEN
THE GRADUATION CEREMONY

*Light up your candles today,
so your tomorrow will be illuminated.*

Two days before graduation, I requested for my typed speech from my secretary for editing. "I haven't typed it yet ma." She responded. "What do you mean you haven't typed it? I gave it to you a week ago;" was my response. However, I reconsidered knowing how busy we all have been; therefore, we both agreed she'd get to it immediately. In this chapter, I have a combo testimony, a two-part testimony. First, is about the God sent wind. Second, is about the graduation speech.

A few weeks before the graduation, the leadership of the student council came to me with a special request. They explained to me about an established history of rainfall on their graduation ceremony day. They understand July is rainy season; but if it was okay with me, they want to put what I have been teaching them to practice. "And what is that?" I asked. Their leader started, "you told us that there is nothing God cannot do. He can change any situation. We want God to hold the rain so it will not fall until after the ceremony."

I listened attentively. He continued, "this is our plan, we have decided to fast and pray for three days." In response to their request, I told them I'd join them. A few days before the graduation day, the fasting and prayer was observed by the students and willing staff members.

On that graduation day, God clearly answered our prayers. The sun shined with low humidity and clear sky. Then, the wonder of all, during the ceremony, just before my speech, God's presence majestically dropped in, in the arena. We didn't understand what it was until later.

The ceremony was in a very big field, well decorated with all kinds of ornaments, ribbons, balloons and so forth. The decorators made a centerpiece like a tower well designed with decorative ornaments. Little did we know that the agents of Satan had used the centerpiece to plant evil thing for whatever purpose. On the program, just before my speech, a mighty wind came with force, accompanied with raindrops that fell like hail from heaven. The wind blew away the centerpiece far from the field. The wind and the raindrops lasted for no more than a minute. The sun was still shining the same. There were no thunderstorms nor Lightening. The arena became a little noisy, because people marveled at what just happened. Later, we discovered there was no raindrops on the ground, on the east or west of the town; it happened only within the surrounding of that arena. The band played for few minutes for people to settle down.

Chapter Twelve

Before I continue with the second part of this testimony, I want to make it clear that all parties involved in the wrongdoing in both part one and two were all forgiven long time ago. I am only giving these testimonies to glorify my God for His goodness.

On that graduation day, it was obvious that the enemy was at war; but I will not glorify the devil by enumerating the wrongs of that day. However, I will not fail to mention that up to when I got to the arena, not only was my speech not still typed, but my hand-written copy was missing. Between my personal assistant and my secretary, they found two pages of the six-page handwritten speech. I convinced myself I have no choice but to deliver an impromptu speech.

After the wind, as I stepped out to the middle of the field, I observed a solemn tranquility in the arena. Within me, I felt an unusual calmness in my nerves. For a moment, I looked around without a word and smiled. After recognizing every individual present, my speech started with, the wonders of our God— in adoration to our creator.

In summary, my speech broadly talked about the uniqueness and the meaningfulness of every individual on planet earth. Our purpose here individually and together. No matter where we find ourselves, no matter what position or assignment entrusted to us, we need to serve selflessly with every bone in our being. We need to serve with honesty, care, and dignity. "Observe your environment, ask yourselves what can I do to make my community better? Ask what more can I do for my people? Make every individual feel he/she matters. Let the people you encounter know they are important and valuable."

Learn to disagree with respect. Honor each other's values. Our values showcase our uniqueness as a people. Above all, listen to one another, especially to the children. We must be guided by the plans of making the world a better place tomorrow. To achieve peace and unity tomorrow, we must love today by preparing our future generations. Our children and our youths must be taught, and must learn today; so, they can have direction with purpose to become better leaders and citizens of tomorrow. Always strive to do the right thing no matter your age nor the situation.

Be willing to compromise your opinions with others' when necessary; but, never compromise your integrity. Your integrity will make you stand out from the crowd.

Next, I focused on the 300 plus students/pupils that were graduating that day and their peers that filled the arena. I spoke to them about preparation, how they have stepped one step up the ladder of success in their journey into the world.

It was one of the best speeches I ever delivered at the time. However, I did not realize how good it was, until I watched it on the video. The audience appeared marinated with the presence of our creator as they listened. The words were flowing out of my mouth like a breeze from a steady wind. Towards the end of my speech, I told them my pledge to the Almighty God; then I asked, what about you?

The audience comprised of pupils, students, parents, guardians, grandparents, teachers of every level of education, including university lecturers, pastors, to local government officials, Chiefs and High Chiefs, dignitaries, including managers and leaders of governmental and non-governmental organizations, and of course, thousands of children, youths and young adults.

Chapter Twelve

In an orderly manner, as if I had planned it, I faced each group and asked them if they want to join the band of making our world a better place by preparing our children now, to become better leaders and citizens of tomorrow. As I raised my hand, all educators, pastors, counselors and all that had anything to do with influencing children, raised up their hands too as they repeated the pledge after me. Secondly, the parents, guardians and caregivers. Finally, the students and pupils. Before the pledge, I asked them— the children, if they are willing to receive the love and to love and respect others around them. Most importantly, I urged them to honor their creator.

As I watched the video and saw the attentiveness of the audience, the tears of joy, the smile with the repeated applause of the audience throughout the speech, captivated me so much that that speech, became the beginning of this book, *My Pledge!* I believe the success of this speech was because the audience saw that the words, the message was coming out from my innermost heart, and it was genuine. It was no written fancy speech that I just had to read to score points; it was real. Therefore, they connected, genuinely connected. They all reciprocated because there was none that was left out. Looking at them also, I realized they were not only touched by the words, but were feeling the presence of God too.

I closed my speech with these words: "As human beings, we cannot find our road map, not to talk of getting to our destination without first identifying who we are, why we are here, what is our purpose on planet earth, and how to accomplish it. We must realize that we cannot accomplish our purpose alone; we need other human beings to achieve and excel.

Without others, we are nobody, with no destination. We should have dreams that will accommodate and add value to others; most importantly, have dreams big enough that God can use to accomplish His purpose through you."

While you're on this stage of life, perform your best to leave a lasting memory of your legacy that conforms to human integrity, an integrity that showcases kindness, caring and loving. When you get off the stage, the lasting memory you'd leave for all that watched your life on the stage would be joy, happiness and peace.

Alone, we accomplish little; but together, we will make greater impacts. Know this: a life without dream is meaningless; and a life without a purpose is not worth living.

Children, light up your candles today so your tomorrow will be illuminated.

CHAPTERTWELVE

Alone, we accomplish little; but together, we will make greater impacts. Know this: A life without dream is meaningless; and a life without a purpose is not worth living. Children, light up your candles today so your tomorrow will be illuminated.

Chapter Thirteen

REACHING OUTSIDE THE BOX

All children belong to God.

In the beginning of this book I wrote: *"A child asks: Who can change my tomorrow today?"* In order to explain what I mean by reaching outside the box, I'd like to share with you two articles I wrote in 2008 and 2009.

THE UNNOTICED

The Unnoticed, written on January 17, 2008 about a boy I call Willie.

Willie is a seven-year-old orphan begging on the street of Ikeja, Lagos, Nigeria. At 6AM Willie is sent to the street by his employer to go to the roadside and beg instead of going to school. At 11AM he takes a bucket of bags of pure water on his head moving from one car to another, hocking the bags of chilled, pure water. By 4PM he returns to begging.

Most days Willie starves until evening before he eats his one meal a day, Garri with a small lump of meat, according to my sources. However, on rare occasions, his employer would give him either one comb of corn or two slices of bread with water at midday. Any day that Willie did not bring good returns to his employer either by begging or through the sale of bags of pure water, he receives a beating.

One fateful day Willie was not feeling fine, and he told his boss he could not go to work. Instead of taking Willie to the hospital for treatment, the boss ushered him to work. Little Willie sat on the street corner weeping with a fever, and nobody noticed him. Willie, even though very young, remembered his mother when she was alive, how she used to bathe him and took him to his nursery school. He used to have breakfast before going to school, and his mother would give him a lunch box with food for his lunch. In addition, she'd give him money most of the time for his snacks. Today Willie is in the streets of Ikeja, Lagos sitting and crying all alone, and nobody cares or notices. What will be the future of Willie? How can an adult abuse a child as young as Willie? and nobody either notices or cares enough to report to the officials. How long will this continue?

Willie cries and nobody hears. He sits in agony; he hocks and begs on the street and people pretend not to see. The society is busy. Money is flowing from one corner to another, but nothing comes to Willie.

Chapter Thirteen

Willie's Cry...
Mama, mama, why did you leave me?
Mama, take me to your world.
My world is wicked,
I hate my existence in it.
It looks beautiful in my eyes,
But in my heart, it's so ugly.
Mama, you told me about God.
Tell Him, if He can see me
I need His help now.
I'll wipe His feet with tears of joy.
He should take me to heaven.
Do not delay mama, I miss you so much.

"He who has pity on the poor lends to the Lord, And He will pay back what he has given." Proverbs 19:17.

People of the world, look around you. What do you see, and who do you see? What are you going to do about it? It does not matter who you are or what you are, there's always something you can do for somebody, a child or even for your environment, to make a change for the better. Ask yourself, what is your call? What can you contribute to humanity?

Children are blessings from God. Also, without children, there will be no future; therefore, embrace the blessings of children whether they're yours or not. Take care of the children. Perhaps some of them are angels within. When we love and care for them, God will shower his blessings upon us and our households unceasingly.

REACHING OUTSIDE THE BOX

Those at the top, either in the government or any organization that can render a helping hand, don't just allocate, ensure that the allocation gets to the appropriate individuals; be it within the educational system, community, or special homes such as the orphanages. Do not delegate without proper supervision. The children are counting on you; don't let them down, don't let God down, and especially don't deprive yourselves of God's blessings.

Look for the lost children and bring them back home. Children like Willie need your help. It's high time you opened your eyes and do something. Identify your purpose and make a difference in humanity.

"He who has my commandments and keeps them, it is he who loves me. And he who loves Me will be loved by My Father, and I will love him and manifest Myself to him."

—*John 14:21 NKJV*

"And this commandment we have from Him: that he who loves God must love his brother also."

—*1 John 4:21 NKJV*

This article was written in 2008, but situations like Willie's still exist around the world, especially in Africa. It is children like Willie and some of the questions I have asked throughout this book that moved me into children and youth ministry, a platform in which I am provided with the opportunity to help educate and provide for some orphans, and other children from impoverished homes through scholarship awards.

The crusade of reaching out to needy children is beyond a handful of persons. It is a crusade for all. In one way or

Chapter Thirteen

the other, we can extend our godly love and blessings to our future generations by letting them know they matter, and they are valuable. The love we give today will multiply from generation to generation. In other words, the seed of love we plant in this generation will yield the fruits of the spirit in the future generations

"Remember, a life without a purpose is not worth living."

My Pledge!

"IN THE RIVER THEY SWIM"

Once in time, I went off on a journey very far away in search for wisdom. Years later, I became homesick, then, I decided to return to my familiar environment. Upon arrival, I noticed a familiar ground, but it was no longer the home I remembered and yearned for.

I walked, gazing and wondering what might have happened to my home. I saw no one; but suddenly, I heard a voice very faint and weary coming from the riverside.

Hence, I discovered that COHISA, my Alma Matter had fallen off the Boat; deep inside the river are her children swimming, crying and clenching for an anchor, but to no avail. Alas! Her mother could bear it no longer; so, she lamented.

COHISA! COHISA!! COHISA!!!
The Great Varsity!
How could the world watch you sink inside the deep River?
You the taproot of a big tree,
Your strength draws water to the tree.
You provide nourishment to the branches and leaves.
They survive because of you;
They show off their beauty to the world pretending—you do not exist.
If only they could remember...
Just to remember to say, thank you.

Chapter Thirteen

Gazing at the river, I was overshadowed with the feeling of empathy, as I watched the children struggling and crying in the river, as they swim helplessly. Suddenly, my conscious self re-emerged in me; then, **I realized that nothing I could do alone would save my Alma Matter and her children.** But, I remembered that COHISA was once a very renowned Post Primary Institution. Who produced numerous intellectuals who are blessed and scattered all around the world.

Therefore, I invited and urged my comrades to join hands in rescuing our Alma Matter from the river, and not to allow it to be either relegated nor vanished forever.

In the gathering I highlighted the problems of our Alma Matter to the old students, that **our Alma Matter, COHISA, has become a "No-Man's-Land".** Students no longer feel safe in their own domain. The image of the school had gone down the drain due to the dilapidated buildings, unsafe and unsecured environment.

According to the Principal of the school, a security guard was murdered within the school premises not too long ago. School properties are looted and even some portion of the land have been taken and sold by land speculators, thereby subjecting the school authorities to constant embarrassment. Moreover, some of the school's dormitories have been turned into a dump and lavatory by outsiders.

I reminded the ex-students that this great Institution is the foundation of what we are today and whatever we may become tomorrow. **It's high time we put our candle light up on the table for the world to see;** hence, COHISA needs our help. In lure of my address to my former school mates, I remembered the beginning, how I became a member of this great Institution.

In 1973, 1 sat for an entrance examination in this premise. As I was standing near the school's Library after the exams, a tall handsome man walked towards me and greeted. "What is your name?" He asked. I told him my name. He again asked, "Are you a sister to…? (He mentioned my brother's name), I responded "yes sir." He then asked a third question, "Are you as intelligent as your brother?" My response was— "I believe so". He smiled and gave me a hug.

He also introduced himself as the Principal of the school. This man went around to greet and chat with every candidate within the perimeter. No matter your answer, he had something funny to say.

I may have sounded smart to him, but the truth is that I was no way as intelligent as my elder brother. Yet, I was very eager to become a part of that great Institution. **I went home that day feeling very special and I prayed like I never prayed before for God to help me become a member of the COHISA family.**

It did not take me long during my first year in COHISA, to discover that the warm friendly environment I experienced in the day of my entrance exams was "a way of life in COHISA. The principal of the school recognized and identified every student by name. He had a great rapport with both his students and his faculty members. His unique intellectual abilities and style of leadership was uncommon.

If caring was not instilled in us during our pre-High school years, it was certainly instilled in us during our

CHAPTER THIRTEEN

High School years at COHISA VARSITY. The question now is, what happened to us after graduating from COHISA? Did we leave our hearts behind? Where is it written that you must have surplus before you can remember the people next to you or the people you left behind? As we continue in our daily quest for success, please, let us remember to show gratitude to God and benevolence to mankind by giving a little percentage of our wealth, time and talents to the people we left behind, and to our Alma Matter, COHISA. This was my plea to my comrades. I precisely urged them to recount their blessings and express their gratitude to God by sharing their blessings with others, especially the children swimming in the river crying for help. These are the poor students in this public school. "In the river, they swim", and cannot reach a dry land to anchor.

Their parents cannot afford to send them to good private schools. Public schools are all they've got. My brothers and sisters all over the world, help to create a dry land for these children swimming in the river.

The conclusion of my address during the COHISA WORLD WIDE Convention reads: **"I have a vision that our home which was invaded and destroyed by unidentified aliens will soon be restored back to its original glory.** Hence, this invitation of brotherhood to come together in unity, to make a difference in our community, to contribute to the growth, welfare of humanity, and to make this world a better place." Shortly after the convention, the school compound was fenced and most of the buildings renovated. Furthermore, the current Governor of our state at the time, embarked on building of modern schools, and my Alma Matter is one of the selected schools to benefit on the embarked modern school projects. Glory Be to God.

I entitled the address as "A Call of Need" in 2003 when the convention took place. Among the dignitaries in the convention were government and private organizations' Executives, current and former state commissioners, Royal Highnesses, Chiefs and High Chiefs, leaders, managing directors and many others from all over the state and a few coming from outside the state.

In this gathering, I will not fail to mention that two of the former Principals of this great institution and the current Principal at the time, who was also a graduate of that High School were honored with plaques of honor for their services to humanity. The grand honor was to the Principal I met on my entrance examination day in 1973. This man educated several generations of students who are intellectuals all over the world today.

I decided to include this article here in this book because, the situation described in this article is still preeminent in several nations of this world. Hence, the plea in the address applies to every human being on earth. Our Lord commanded us first to love God. Second, to love our neighbors as ourselves; which includes caring for the poor and the needy. More importantly, we should not ignore nor maltreat the children, for they are our future.

Never say that's not my child. All children belong to God; and He mandates us to care for them as ours. Therefore, do this and God will reward you with abundance of blessings.

CHAPTER THIRTEEN

THE ORIGINAL COHISA POEM

Source: "A CALL OF NEED" An Address by Fyne C. Ogonor, the Organizer, and the Chief Coordinator of the 1st COHISA VARSITY Worldwide Convention; 2003.

COHISA! COHISA!! COHISA!!!
The Great Varsity!
How could the world watch you sink inside the deep Ocean?
You the taproot of a big tree,
Your strength draws water to the tree.
You provide nourishment to the branches and leaves.
They survive because of you;
They show off their beauty to the world pretending—you do not exist.
If only they could remember…
Just to remember to say, thank you.

We must realize that we cannot accomplish our purpose alone; we need other human beings to achieve and excel. Without others, we are nobody, with no destination. We should have dreams that will accommodate and add value to others; most importantly, have dreams big enough that God can use to accomplish His purpose through you.

Chapter Fourteen

DARE TO BELIEVE, MY GOD IS REAL!

"If God is for us, who can be against us?"

The word of God encourages us to be thankful in every situation. This is one principle I have grown to learn, through my life experiences, to uphold; because it gives me balance.

As a result, in every situation, I express my gratitude to God in words of music and poetry. In this chapter, I'll like to share with you more samples of my inspirational poems in my journey of storms and trials of this world. "If God is for us, who can be against us?" There's no God like Jehovah, The Almighty.

HEAVENLY GAZE

A Prayer of Confidence

In the midst of the clouds, I gazed up in the heavens to
seek the face of my God.
Down below is full of distress, calamities
upon calamities,
I refuse to look down because I know my help
comes only from above.
The giants below hound me and did everything
to pull me down.
But I refuse to look down because I hear my Lord
calling for me.
And I know that my help will come only from above.
The dinosaurs of earth threaten to devour me,
But I must not be afraid.
I am covered with the blood of Jesus.
I am protected by the highest power under and above
the universe.
I belong to Jesus Christ.
I will continually praise His name until the dawn
of the day.
Therefore, Lord Jesus,
Adjoin my heart with Thee,
For there's no other way for me, but Thine.
Amen.

Chapter Fourteen

ORDERED STEPS

An ordered step I request from You, Lord!
You are the only one I want to listen to.
The world is full of discouragement, anguish, and pain;
But I am convinced that You are on my side.
Help me Lord not to depart from Your presence.
An ordered step I request from You.
O God when You speak to me,
Turn the volume up so I can hear You.
When You speak,
put conviction in my heart to know You are the one.
Give me understanding to know what You say to me.
Then lead the way so I can follow.
Sometimes I hear a still voice in my heart,
I Wondered, is it You Lord speaking to me?
Or is it just my heart wondering on facts of life?
Dear Lord, speak to me, and
Let me recognize Your voice.
So, there'll be no doubt in my heart,
You're leading my way.

GOD'S PRESENCE

An Affirmation of Faith

God's presence is always with me. My being matters to God.
He was in my yesterday during my dark and bright moments.
Yesterday was full of memories, good and bad,
But I'm glad it's over.
I arrived today with great expectations, hope, and enthusiasm.
Though the path is filled with challenges, troubles and
temptations, I will not be afraid, nor be discouraged.
Even in a strong wind, I will trust my God.
Wherever the wind carries me,
I know God's hands will be there to catch me.
Although, I cannot see tomorrow from here,
But one thing I know for sure, is that when I get there,
My Lord will still be there waiting for me.
God's presence is always with me.

Having a guaranteed safety with God does not mean when you see a fire burning, you'd walk into the furnace because you feel spiritually proof, it will not harm you. Also, it does not mean taking yourself to a lion's den parked with wild lions ready to devour flesh and blood. And you say, what can they do to me? The Lord is with me!

Chapter Fourteen

Our God defiles pride and arrogance; but He adores humility.

However, if the enemies gather and plot against you and say, we will throw him\her into the lion's den and let the lions feed on her. Guess what God will do for you? He will put all the lions to sleep; and when they wake up, He will make them your friends. He did it for prophet Daniel.

Whereas the enemies' plot is to throw you in a furnace of fire, even if they succeed in throwing you inside the fire, it will only happen so our God can be glorified. Yet, the heat in the fire will be converted to air condition. Remember, our God did it for the three Hebrew brothers—Shadrach, Meshack and Abednego. The God of yesterday, is the same God today, and He will be forever. He is the beginning and the end, the Alpha, and the Omega, the first and the last. He is the Creator of the Universe. Hallelujah!

Now you tell me, if the Sovereign and Almighty God is with you, and always on your side, who can be against you? Is there any power greater than His? Absolutely none.

He commands us to be diligent; Watch out for the enemy—the old Devil, who's always ready to steal, kill and devour.

We have our confidence in the Lamb that was sacrificed on the cross of Calvary, whose blood gave us victory, power and authority over the devil; to trample him under our feet. We have our protection insurance; the anointing of our roaring Lion of Judah, whose holiness and presence in our lives give us the assurance of joy, peace on earth, and hope for life eternal.

Children of God, Believe! As long as the Almighty God is on your side, in the precious name of our Lord Jesus Christ, no weapon fashioned against you shall prosper. He will save you from all troubles. This is a guaranteed promise from our heavenly Father. This is His covenant with us.

Believe! Believe! Work your faith, and trust God with no reservations. Doing this, the promises of God will come alive in your life. And all will be well with you.

On this note, I'd like to conclude with the same question I asked in the beginning: A child asks, who can change my tomorrow today?

We must learn to embrace one another. Inside every human being is a fragile flower that sometimes needs to be watered with love. Purposely dish out kind words to others, it will go a long way in buttering someone's rough day. But seek not love from the wrong hearts. Total fulfillment of life — joy, peace and happiness can only be achieved through the acceptance of our creator, God.

I've been favored to experience God's miracles so many times in my life. The love He showers on the imperfect 'me,' gives me the assurance that God will never break a covenant. He honors them.

My prayer is that, the grace of God upon my life should help me always to honor my covenant with my heavenly Father, too.

CHAPTER FOURTEEN

Believe!
Work your faith,
Trust God.

Dear Lord,
"Keep a song
in my heart."

Chapter Fifteen

EPILOGUE

Standing on God's promises

This book, *My Pledge!*, breaks down the understanding of the human belief system in a Supreme Power that emphasizes faith and love.

As children of God on planet earth, we must know our mission in life. The life that spells out the deeper meaning of our existence—to love, care for God's creations, serve, disciple mankind, and worship the Most High God.

We need one another to maximize our potential in existence as humans. Also, as children of the Most High God, we need to rise above all odds, knowing, although we are in this world, we are not *of* this world. Accept the grace of God through our Lord Jesus Christ, and strive to live right by Him. Focus on God's goodness; separate yourselves from the wrongs of this world! Darkness cannot coexist with light. Hatred has no room in the mansion of love. Embrace love; live it, for our God is love, merciful and gracious. Let's keep our hearts in tune with the Lord, for there's no filth in purity. Hence, there's no evil where goodness reigns.

The stories I have told in this book is only a summary of the events as they occurred. I just want my readers to know that the power of prayers cannot be underrated at any time.

Every breath we take should be praises and worship to our God. In other words, every aspect of our lives, and our actions must reverend God. We should open our hearts for the indwelling of the Holy Spirit so we can hear God and obey Him. In addition, we have no reason to be afraid if we know our identity—the Children of the Most High God.

As a child of God, I know His promises to me will never go void. He promised me that no weapon fashioned against me shall prosper. Furthermore, He said He's my refuge and my fortress; He would not allow any evil to befall me nor my household. And that He will save me from all my troubles. This means as long as I seek shelter under His wings and trust Him, no matter the evil or trouble that may come my way, He will rescue me. He clearly stated that, He will deliver me from all troubles, not some. Is there a more guaranteed promise of love than this? All these grace and love is because of the sacrifice on the Cross of Calvary. Glory be to my Lord Jesus, my only Savior and Redeemer. I said previously, during the armed robbery, that it seemed somebody was inside of me acting on my behalf. Yes, there was! The God in me—The Holy Spirit, was in control of the situation. Also, in the devil's midnight visit, the Holy Spirit still removed fear from me.

In conclusion, we must honor God with our trust and obedience to His word. He already assured us of His blessings even when times are hard.

Chapter Fifteen

There is only one living God—Jehovah, the Almighty God; The Creator of the Universe; The Beginning and The End. For this reason, my pledge is to live for Jesus forever; because His grace is sufficient for me. What about you?

*If you haven't accepted Jesus yet, all you must do is humbly bow
and say: My Father in Heaven;
or Dear God, forgive my sins.
Allow the Holy Spirit to teach me your path;
and give me the grace to be obedient
In Jesus name I ask. Amen.*

*If you said this prayer, you are saved.
Join a bible-based Church and be baptized.
Live for Jesus, and do right by Him always.*

REFERENCES

Chapter 1 & 2 ——————————————Proverbs 22: 6

Chapter 6 ————————————————Ecclesiastes 3:1, 2

Chapter 7 ——————————————————Philippians 4: 13

Chapter 9 ———————————Webster's dictionary & Oxford Advanced Learner's dictionary. Prayer defined.

Chapter 10 ——————————————————James 5: 16

Chapter 11 ——————————————————Isaiah 54:17

Chapter 13 ——————————————————Proverbs 19:17, John 14: 21, 1 John 4: 21 Revelation 22:13.

Addresses: ————————————————A Call of Need. My Pledge ! What's Yours?

Author's Profile

Fyne C. Ogonor was born and brought up in Rivers State, Nigeria.

After High School, she traveled to the United States of America, where she earned her Bachelor of Arts degree with honors, from Huston-Tillotson University in Austin, Texas. She later earned a dual MBA degree in Management and Marketing from Mercer University in Atlanta, Georgia, U.S.A..

Fyne is an entrepreneur, an educator, an inspirational speaker, and a writer. She is also the author of "A Moving Train."

Fyne and her husband, Vincent Ogonor, are blessed with five amazing children – Valerie, Ronald, Bryan, Jessica and Stephanie, her motivators and cheerleaders.

Graduation ceremony

Growing up and

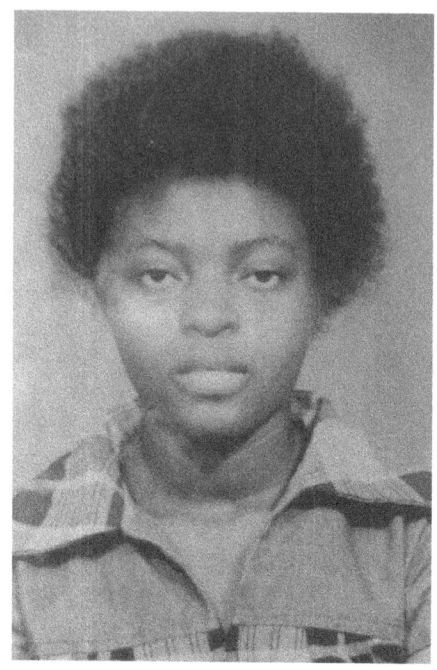

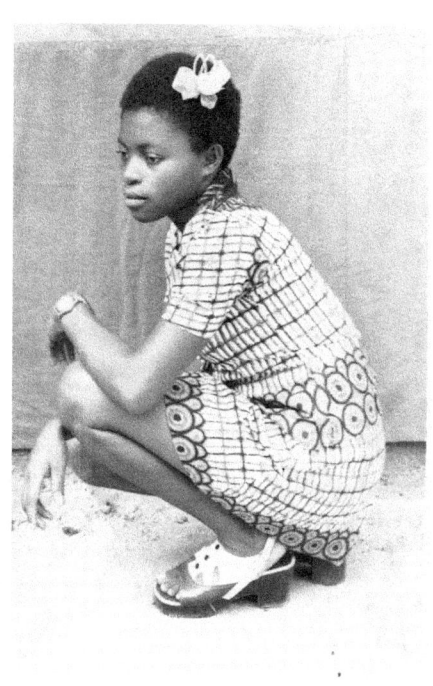

the COHISA DAYS

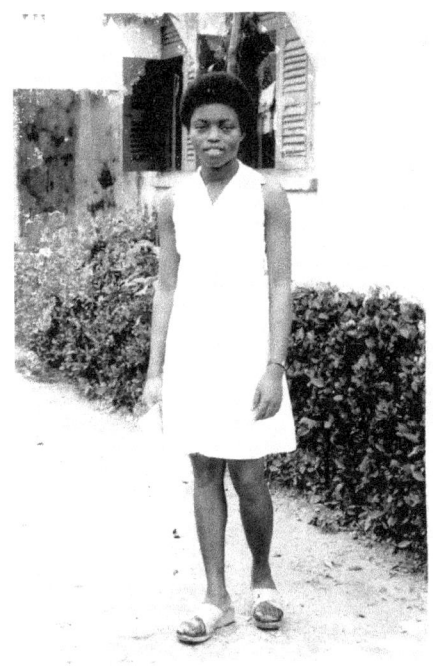

Bye-bye Africa

Hello America!

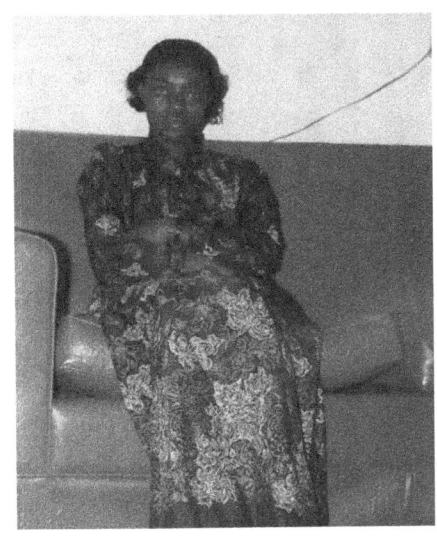

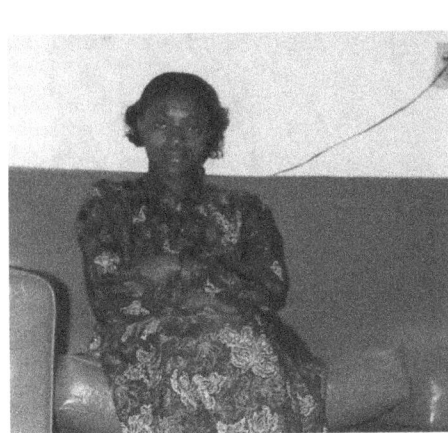

1st COHISA Worldwide Convention

www.ingramcontent.com/pod-product-compliance
Lightning Source LLC
Chambersburg PA
CBHW070723240426
43673CB00003B/121